The Bright Kid Challenge

Ending Conflict and Unlocking the Potential of Smart, Challenging Children

Andrew Fuller

Includes a Teachers' Supplement

SOURCEBOOKS, INC.
NAPERVILLE, ILLINOIS

Published by Sourcebooks, Inc.
P.O. Box 4410, Naperville, Illinois 60567-4410
(630) 961-3900
Fax: (630) 961-2168
www.sourcebooks.com

Originally published in Australia by Finch Publishing Pty Ltd., 2007.

Library of Congress Cataloging-in-Publication Data

Fuller, Andrew.
  [Tricky kids]
  The bright kid challenge : ending conflict and unlocking the potential of
smart, challenging children / Andrew Fuller.
      p. cm.
  Originally published: Tricky kids. Sydney: Finch Pub., 2007.
  "Includes a teachers' supplement."
  Includes bibliographical references and index.
  1. Problem children—Behavior modification. 2. Problem children—
Education. I. Title.
  HQ773.F85 2008
  649'.64—dc22
                          2008018102

Printed and bound in the United States of America
VP 10 9 8 7 6 5 4 3 2 1

*For Vicki and for all the bright kids and their parents
who taught me how to write this book*

Contents

Introduction: born to be wild!

Looking for adventure ... or whatever comes their way

Stubborn, pigheaded, defiant, oppositional, free-ranging, having a mind of their own, iron-willed, forceful, determined, hard-headed, free-spirited, or just plain difficult—call them what you will, there are some kids who are incredibly difficult to raise well.

Compliant, agreeable, sweet children are easy. Parenting them just seems to happen. It evolves. You can see how the wind shifts and set your course accordingly.

Not so with bright kids. Successfully parenting them takes a degree of strategic planning equivalent to sailing around the world. You need to know in advance when to batten down the hatches, when to bail out, and when to sail straight into the eye of the storm.

Having a compliant child is a lesson that there is love in the world. Having a forceful child teaches you that there is still a dark side to be overcome.

Some of the common things parents say that indicate they have a bright child include:

"It doesn't matter what I say ..."

"She just gets something into her mind and won't give it up."

"Some days I could just scream at them ..."

"He has always got to have the last word."

"She's fine when she gets her own way."

"He can argue for hours."

"She just won't take no for an answer."

Do any of these comments sound familiar? If so, congratulations, it's likely you have a bright child. Not always the easiest to parent, in fact downright difficult at times. But don't worry too much: these children grow up to change the world. They often have leadership qualities in bucket-loads. The big trick is to use their strength of character for good, not evil!

Some news you may not want to hear ...

Bright children don't just grow out of their willful personalities, they either learn to adapt and change, or they torment their families for years. Children's characters are relatively stable—it's how you manage their personal style that makes a difference.

Bright kids are the movers and shakers of the future. They know their own mind and have the energy and determination to achieve what they set out to do. These kids do not lack persistence. They are not wishy-washy. They might be wild, difficult, and stressful, but parenting them will teach you a lot about life and about yourself.

Most of the great achievers, politicians, and national figures that are remembered throughout history were forceful children. Sadly, history does not record the thoughts of the parents of Joan of Arc or Alexander the Great as these young adults left home. Did they shed a tear as their children departed, saying, "Hurry home, dear"? Or did they heave a great sigh of relief and think to themselves, "Phew, thank goodness that's over, now they can go and conquer the rest of the world and give us a bit of a break!"? While we might suspect the latter, parenting bright kids can be entertaining.

If you have one of these kids, this book is for you.

About this book

For over 25 years I have been counseling children, young people, and their families. One day—and I'll be the first to admit I was a bit slow on the uptake—I finally realized I was seeing the same kids over and over again. Sure, they had different faces and their own idiosyncrasies and styles, but there were some common themes.

Discussing this further with hundreds of thousands of parents and teachers in seminars has helped me to refine these ideas into a series of recognizable patterns of behavior.

A considerable amount of wailing and gnashing of teeth went into the creation of this book—thankfully, most of it wasn't mine. It was done by the parents and teachers who talked with me about these children, and it is to them that the credit for many of the ideas in this book should go.

More of Andrew's papers, programs and materials can be obtained from www.andrewfuller.com.au

Part One

A SPOTTER'S GUIDE TO BRIGHT KIDS

One of the great paradoxes of life is that many children and adolescents who are difficult to raise and teach often grow up to become, as mentioned, the movers and shakers of the world. They have fantastic energy and leadership potential. During more than 25 years of working with parents and their kids, I have come to realize that, broadly speaking, there are two categories of kids:

1. the lovable, likable, amiable, friendly, compliant kids. You know the ones? You ask them to clean up their room and in a matter of weeks it is done!
2. the fiery ones, the feisty ones, the ones who have a mind of their own. These kids are tricky to parent well. These are the kids that can drive parents mad. These are also the kids with enormous leadership capability. Part One looks at how we can understand these kids in order to steer their energies and optimize their great potential.

1

Ten golden ideas for parenting bright kids

A distressed mother telephoned me. She told me her daughter was pig-headed and stubborn, and had taken to insulting her in public.

"What does she say?" I asked.

The mother replied that her daughter screams out at the top of her voice, "You suck!" The mother sounded desperate and asked for some strategy that might help her daughter. We chatted and thought, and finally we came up with a plan. (The mother phoned me later to let me know the outcome.) On a subsequent occasion in public the daughter once again turned to her mother and screamed out, "You suck!"

At this point the mother turned calmly to her daughter, as we'd worked out over the phone, and said, "No darling, it was you who sucked—you sucked so hard that my nipples ached for hours."

On their way home the daughter muttered to the mother, "If you ever do that to me again ... that was so embarrassing."

Lots of the ideas in this book come from the shifty, cunning strategies parents have used to help their children. Some of the examples are for parenting teenagers, but many are for younger children. I'm sure that as you read these ideas you will come up with even more creative ways to handle situations.

We'll discuss these ideas in greater depth as we go through the book, but these ten golden ideas have been developed by parents who have bright children.

1. They will always outdo you for energy

Bright children have turbo-charged batteries! Any child or teenager has a lot more energy to put into any argument than any adult ever has, and they'll use all of their energy to win a battle. Therefore, wise parents limit the number of areas they want to have a positive effect on. Don't try to do too much.

It's generally a good idea to decide on one behavior you'd like to promote so you can see more of it, and one behavior that you want to try to lessen. Then stick to those two behaviors for a minimum of six weeks. Any more than this and not only will you be an over-achiever, you'll be a nervous, exhausted wreck.

2. Two crocodile brains equals a lot of snapping

When we use brain scans or positron emission tomography (PET) to look in on children's and young people's brains as they engage in conflict, we find very distinct patterns. The two parts of the brain that are really active in conflict situations are the brain stem, which is really about activation, and the amygdala, which is the "do I fight you or run away from you?" part. That's pretty much it!

This means that in the middle of an argument, these kids are about as reasonable as your average crocodile. Rationalizing, discussing, explaining, and reasoning with them in the middle of an argument is often a waste of time. As much as your cherished advice or lecture may feel important, you are wasting your breath. They can't hear your wise words or learn from them when the parts of their brain that control listening and learning aren't active.

When you get steamed up, you also become about as reasonable as your average crocodile. Two crocodiles talking to one another often equals a lot of snapping. If possible, walk away, cool off, calm down, then intervene.

3. Don't mud-wrestle with pigs!

Bright kids love intensity. They like drama, soap operas, grunge, gore, horror, and action. Not only that, they are very, very talented at *creating* drama, horror, and action. As they get lots of drama in their life, they are used to it. Drama and intensity are home base for them.

I always say to parents that arguing with a bright child is a lot like mud-wrestling a pig; you both end up dirty but only the pig is happy. If you want to entertain them by providing an argument or a fight, please go right ahead, but if you really want to help your child learn a broader range of behaviors, we are going to need to find another way.

This doesn't mean parents have to give in to bright children. It does mean they need to be sneakier! Unless you want to mud-wrestle a pig, and thereby entertain your bright child, you are going to have to give up a habit that creeps into the lives of most parents at some stage:

The dangerous art of the provocative question

Yes, the art of the provocative question is a method used by many parents, and it is 100 percent guaranteed to cause an argument.

Examples of provocative questions include:

- "Have you got any homework?"
- "Have you cleaned your room?" (When it's clear she hasn't)
- "You don't think you are going out looking like that, do you?"
- "How many times do I have to tell you?"
- "What were you thinking?"
- "I suppose you can explain why your school report looks like this, can you?"

If you want to get a bright kid into defensive argument mode, ask a provocative question. It will entertain her and exasperate you. It will spark a debate and a conflagration that will last for hours.

Turn provocative questions into definite, clear statements. Some examples are:

- "Okay, it's homework time."

- "Let's get the room cleaned up before dinner."

- "I'd like to remind you of our agreement."

- "Let's chat about how to help you with school."

This leads us to the next golden rule, which is that most parents of bright kids find routines more powerful than words.

4. What you do is more important than what you say

It's not always what you say, it's often what you do. In recent decades there seems to have been a tendency for parents to feel they need to explain everything to their children. While some explanations can be useful, parents have fallen into the trap of believing if they just give their child the right explanation, then all will be well.

This might work well for some children, but bright children often don't stick around long enough to hear the words, or are so busy getting their own point of view across that you just don't get a chance. With bright children, what you do is more important than what you say.

There is very good research that tells us that the small rituals that we put into family life are a powerful positive force. They build goodwill and routine and, with bright children, routines and rituals are good. The rituals don't need to be expensive, in fact the best ones cost very little or nothing. Rituals are the things you regularly do that later on you hope your children will say, "Mom always made sure we did …" or "Dad always involved us in …."

Your rituals will most likely be different from other families'. It might be the Friday night pizza, the Wednesday evening walk after dinner, or the Sunday night movie. A ritual is something you do regularly as a family that does *not* depend on how children are behaving.

> *Rituals act like coat hangers upon which people hang the good memories of their lives.*

When you raise bright children, it is highly likely that your family rituals slip. Time after time I hear parents tell me, "We used to get pizza on Friday nights, but one night he went wild so we stopped that" or "We used to go out together, but she caused such a fuss we stopped it."

If this is true for your family, stop and think about the types of rituals you could start.

Some examples of family rituals

- Monday movie
- Thursday takeaway dinner
- Swimming together at the local pool
- Friday pizza
- Sunday lunch
- Saturday morning clean-up
- Wednesday evening bowling
- Church
- Community functions
- Sports
- Watching some TV shows together (especially if you discuss them afterwards)
- Caring for pets
- Family gatherings

5. Build resilience in your child

Resilience is the happy knack of being able to bungee jump through the pitfalls of life. When tough times come, resilience helps you to rise above adversity and hardship.

Resilience is developed in children and adolescents when they have:

- a sense of being loved by their family,
- a diverse group of friends, and
- an adult outside their family who likes them.

Being loved by their family

You can help your child to be resilient by always making it clear that you love him (even if you are also making it very clear that you don't like the way he is behaving at the moment).

One of the ways of freely expressing love for a bright child is not to give in to the extent that you end up feeling used. Parents who give in too much end up feeling resentful, and feeling used and resentful is corrosive to goodwill in families. If you are feeling this way, stop! Give yourself a break. Be less helpful for a time.

Being a sleep-deprived, stressed-out human being does no one any favors. Parenting bright kids will test the reserves of even the strongest person. Parenting is a marathon, not a sprint, and by looking after yourself, you can give your child what he or she needs as well as ensuring you have the energy to keep going.

The most powerful factor in your child's path towards a great life is his relationship with you. Having a positive, strong bond with you is the top priority. So if either of you is behaving in ways that threaten the strength of that relationship, it is time to work out a different approach.

Seven messages for parents who do too much

1. Remember: one day my child may need to cope without me.

2. Children learn competence and confidence by tackling some things on their own.

3. There are some situations in which my child can cope without my help.

4. Help is not always helpful. Sometimes it robs people of the opportunity to work out their own way of doing things.

5. The toughest trees grow in the windiest conditions. Making everything easy for your child won't help him or her cope with hardship.

6. Rarely or never do anything for a child that he or she can do for him- or herself.

7. Things that are scarce are more valued. While I'm not suggesting you distance yourself from your child, I am suggesting that if you are feeling undervalued or used, make your assistance scarcer.

Having a diverse group of friends

The second resilience factor is friendships. Always look around for opportunities to broaden your child's social friendships. Ideally, try to help your child to develop some friends in school and some out of school. Youth groups, extended family, activity clubs, YMCA/YWCA, church groups, Scouts, camps, and community service organizations all provide great ways of doing this.

It often seems that the bright children who get into big trouble are those who whittle their friendships down to a few similarly inclined young people. Keep them mixing with a range of people.

Some bright children are also loners. While there is nothing wrong with being a loner, getting practice at interacting with a range of people is a good skill for all children to develop. This is particularly true for bright children, who often have only one or two ways of being with people.

An adult outside the family

Raising children is a tricky business. Raising forceful children is a tricky and tiring business. Having an adult outside your family who you can trust to form a positive relationship with your child can make an incredible difference in his life. This other adult shouldn't be involved in disciplining or sorting out problems necessarily, but rather should be someone who your child can go to when he feels unable to go to you.

6. Mind what you do with them just before they go to sleep

What happens just before going to sleep gets processed into long-term dreams. What you say to your child just before she goes to sleep is what she will remember most. So the important message is:

No matter how lousy a day you have had,

No matter what conflicts have occurred,

No matter how many harsh words have been traded,

Find time to make some peace before she goes to sleep.

If you feel that in the turmoil of the day she may have forgotten that you love her, remind her. You are building a bridge of peace and connection that hopefully will reach into the next day.

The old adage of "never go to sleep on a fight" is right.

7. Know their friends (and feed them)

Any parent who knows their child's friendship group is in a powerful position. Parents of bright children need to make sure they know their child's friends and, wherever possible, their child's friends' parents.

What's the best way to get to know kids? Feed them! The barbecue may be your most powerful ally in your attempts to do this.

And the best way to get to know their friend's parents? First, *never* ask your own child permission to contact his friends' parents. Phone them. Introduce yourself. Every chance you get, keep introducing yourself: "Hi, I'm ...'s mom [or dad]. My name is ...."

It might sound a bit basic, but most people live busy lives, and it's not easy to remember your children's friends' parents' names. By being prepared to introduce yourself and keep on re-introducing yourself, you increase the likelihood that if there are ever problems, you will be able to join forces to discuss them.

8. Look out for conversation fuel

Some bright kids can be too easy to talk to when they are angry and incredibly difficult to talk to when they are calm. That is, lots of words can fly around in the middle of an argument, but at the very moments when you do get a chance to build your relationship by having a relaxed chat, they can be as responsive as a house brick.

Look around for conversation fuel. If you can't find much, check in with your child's teacher(s), sports coaches, or her friends' parents. One of the easiest ways to gain fuel for conversation is to notice what television show your child especially likes and to sit down and watch it with her. Spend a few weeks watching it without commenting and then start to use the issues in the show to springboard conversations.

If one of the rituals that has slipped in your house is the family meal without the TV, radio, computer, or another electronic device blaring, turn it off, put on the answering machine, and try to start a conversation. (Of course, if this cuts across the time of the favorite TV show, it may be better to alter the timing of dinner.)

Eating together without the electronic distractions can be scary and unfamiliar for the entire family if it's been a while. One family told me they made a pact for six weeks to try to have at least one meal each day with no electronics. Their first five meals were spent in awkward, uncomfortable silence. Their sixth meal was an argument. It took three long weeks before conversation got beyond the odd grunt.

The point is to be persistent. It's easy for parents to give in to the magnetic attraction that children have for video games, computers, and televisions. Don't get brushed off by the shrugs, the "Dunno's," and the "Nothing's."

9. Timing is everything!

Catch them at the right moment. (We'll talk more about this when we look at mood changing.) It's important to realize that if you see your child in the crashed-out position on the couch, it is probably not the best time to ask him to take out the trash, feed the cat, tickle the goldfish, empty the dishwasher, or repaint the entire house! Wait for those rare moments of verticality, when he is upright and ideally on the move, and then try.

Also, realize that it takes them time to process your requests. If you have teenagers, this is especially important to know. Make a request or a suggestion and then move on. Let the processing begin. It might take a few minutes for an idea to convert into action. An unwise parent makes a request and then waits nearby while their child processes the information. Don't do this. Put in your request and then move away. Return periodically to check on and applaud progress.

For example, you might say, "Please feed the cat," and then move away. Come back after a few minutes and say, "Ah good, you've raised one arm." Leave again. Return after a few minutes and say, "Ah good, the cat is nearby."

One mother recently tried this out. She went

home and said to her daughter, "Please put the trash out," and walked away. There was a deathly silence throughout the house. Not a murmur. Then she heard the back door slam and her daughter said, "I'm not taking out the recycling bin, though!"

10. They need you!

In your darker moments, this might be hard to believe. But they do need you. Bright children probably need more time from their parents than other kids. They need time to feel loved, they need time to learn to curb their more erratic impulses, and they need time to feel they can give something back as well. They may not always give this impression, but they do.

All children fear abandonment. Bright children often fear that they won't be loved if they are not funny, thrill-seeking, determined, wise-cracking, vigilant, or successful enough. Much of their forcefulness is camouflaged fear and worry.

Learning that you are loved for *who you are* rather than for what you do is one of the great lessons of life. Bright children need to learn this lesson, and it is one that only parents can really teach.

> News Flash! Your child does not need you as a friend.
> He or she does need you as a "fierce friend."

A fierce friend

One of the best definitions of good parenting for bright children I have ever come across derives from the Buddhist tradition. It's called "fierce friendship."

A fierce friend is someone who:

- treats their relationship as if there is no way out,
- acts as if they are always on their child's side, and
- is clearly not going to put up with the "BS" the child sometimes puts out.

Hopefully you have a fierce friend in your own life. They are not always the most comfortable person to be around because they will tell you the things about yourself that you sometimes don't want to hear. They are people you can rely on and, when times are tough, are the people you can turn to for help.

Being a fierce friend to your child takes some steely resolve. The first thing to do is to determinedly place yourself at the center of your child's life. Bright kids are talented at maneuvering parents to the sidelines when it suits them. Help them to know that in life, as they are growing up, if they want things to happen, they are going to have to negotiate with you.

It's almost as if you are saying to your child, "Come hell or high water, by hook or by crook, you are going to have to put up with me." While this degree of firmness may sound harsh, it actually reassures the child and helps her to form a solid base through her relationship with you. What you are really saying to your child is, "Whatever happens, I will not give up on you." This is certainty as important for teenagers as it is for younger children.

The second characteristic of fierce friends is that they are always on your side. They are your biggest supporter. Bright kids have a talent for extracting the worst from some adults— adults who will want to cajole, control, and coerce them. Unfortunately, these kids will have plenty of opportunities to perceive the world as a fairly hostile and punishing place. They need an antidote to this. The antidote is you.

Being your child's biggest supporter means focusing more on her strengths and positives than on her irritating behaviors. It means when she does "lose it," you are there to say, "Don't worry, I know you'll get past this." Bright kids need your love most when they deserve it least.

In counseling sessions, bright kids often comment on the power that their parent's belief in them has. One young adult reflected to me, "I really wanted to get into a life of crime and drugs, but my mother kept telling me she believed in me and loved me, and I just couldn't let her down."

Being a fierce friend also means helping your child to avoid some negative outcomes. Swooping her up or distracting her and moving her out of harm's way are important strategies.

There is a school of thinking in parenting books that parents should let natural consequences apply. For example, if a child doesn't put clothes in the hamper, the parent doesn't wash the clothes, and eventually the child will learn to put their clothes in the hamper. This is logical, and works for many families.

But when you have a bright kid, this type of parenting doesn't work. The extreme nature of her behaviors means we need to find faster ways of intervening. Letting natural consequences apply might mean that your child finds out that if she loses her cool or has tantrums in social situations, people won't want to be with her. If you sit back and allow this type of learning to happen, by the time the lesson has been learned, she won't have any friends. Letting natural consequences apply for bright kids would be like allowing your child to play on the road so she can learn that trucks might run her over.

As we'll see in later chapters, we need to be much more tuned in to their dance steps.

If you are flying solo ...

Parenting bright kids can be enormously hard work at times. They have a power to divide and conquer even the most stoic of couples and leave them bickering and squabbling. If you are a single parent of a bright kid, some of the challenges will be amplified.

Here are some hints for the single parents of bright kids:

- *Get enough sleep.* The boundless energy of some bright kids means you'll become exhausted. Set rock-solid bedroom and sleep routines. Read carefully the sections on sleep later in this book.

Have some cavalry to call. There will be days when you regard yourself as an absolute failure as a parent. Ask someone you trust to be your sounding board. Phone them and ask for advice. Use them as a parent coach. This doesn't mean you always need to take their advice, but it will help you clarify in your own mind what to do.

Keep your friends. Bright kids can be difficult to manage in social settings and can alienate people. Some of your friends will be understanding about the challenges facing you, others will be less child-friendly. Work out who belongs to which category, and know who you can invite on outings with your children and who you should catch up with in a child-free zone.

Not every battle needs to be won. Single parents can't afford the energy to argue every point with bright kids. Many bright kids love family dramas, which entertain them and frustrate you. Take some time to think of the five most important things you want your child(ren) to gain from your parenting. For example, some parents will choose issues like school completion, honesty, being a good friend, doing what you say you are going to do, or treating other people as you like to be treated. Once you've worked out your priority areas, focus fairly exclusively on them. These are the issues you must be prepared to battle for. For most other issues, take your sail out of their winds.

Find an activity that helps you clear your head and straighten out your thinking. Having a small ritual that gives you even a little bit of time for yourself each day allows you to regain perspective.

Guard new romances. Bright kids can be so used to exerting power in their families that they can feel extremely threatened if their parent meets someone new. Their behavior can intensify and quickly crush a fledgling romance. It's probably best to keep potential new partners away from bright kids while you build and strengthen that new relationship.

> ▪ *You are the parent.* If you do form a new relationship, don't allow your new partner to parent your bright kid. New partners often want to be helpful and protective. This means they may be tempted to intervene if your bright kid gives you a hard time. Don't let them do this. It will build resentment in your bright kid and possibly in your new relationship as well. Turn to your newly beloved and sweetly let him or her know that you want them as your lover, not as a back-up parent.

The following chapters

Bright children are, of course, individuals. They remain steadfastly, doggedly true to themselves. Nevertheless, in working with children and adolescents over many years, several main patterns do seem to occur over and over again.

While your child may not fit neatly into one type, it is worth reading through the following chapters to help you identify common behaviors and strategies. The idea is not to describe your child to a "T," but to give you some ideas about effective strategies.

Bright kids have patterns of behavior that can become as regular as a dance routine. The problem is that when a bright kid starts a dance routine, the whole family all too often tiptoes through the steps. Rather than being run around in circles, these chapters try to acquaint you with some of the common dance numbers and give you a few good moves of your own.

Instead of trying to classify your child precisely as one type or another, the more important question to ask yourself is, "What sort of parent does my child need me to be?"

Not everyone is going to like the following descriptions. They are confronting and, while at first you might read them as being too negative, I think it is important to take an honest look at what different types of kids often do and how we can help them.

One of the common problems faced by bright children (and forceful people, for that matter) is that they become one-trick ponies. They have one way of interacting with the world, and that's it. Being forceful personalities means they are often very successful with the strategies they use. The problem can be that the strategy is so successful, they don't learn any others.

Parents know that their child needs to learn a range of ways of dealing with the world if he is to succeed and be resilient.

Takeaways

- Parenting bright kids requires a clear-headed strategy.
- Plan your campaign tactics with as much care as a master strategist.
- Learn the art of conflict avoidance.
- Steer clear of provocative questions.
- With bright kids, routines have more power than words.

2

The Manipulators

Motto:

Whatever
it takes

Mascots

Angelica from *Rugrats*: cunning, conniving, and crafty, she loves to set up her cousins and friends.

Queen Elizabeth I: her mother, Anne Boleyn, was beheaded by her father, Henry VIII, and she was imprisoned by her half-sister, Mary, who she in turn had executed. As England's first long-serving female monarch, for years she had to watch her back and play various factions off against each other.

Henry Kissinger: as National Security Advisor to President Nixon, Kissinger arranged Nixon's famous summit visits to China and the Soviet Union in 1972. These visits sought to defuse tension between the U.S. and the Communist powers.

Dick Cheney: as U.S. Vice President, he has overseen the wars in Afghanistan and Iraq. He was CEO of Haliburton Energy Services, which has gained many lucrative contracts to help rebuild Iraq.

Manipulators are kids who can wrap adults around their little finger, eat them for breakfast, hoodwink, and charm the socks off them. Manipulators often dominate and control other people. In some instances they bully other children but are very, very good at playing cute to adults.

The best mascot I can think of for the Manipulators comes from the children's television show *Rugrats.* If you haven't seen Angelica from *Rugrats,* you have really missed something. The Manipulators of this world are anything but angels, and they can be boys as well as girls.

Characteristics and behaviors

Manipulators are determined characters who are often extremely successful long-term in business and corporate life. They are quite often single-minded people who like to take charge and tell people what to do. Hopefully they don't end up being your boss. Also, I'm not sure you would want them running a nursing home where you are being cared for in your older years.

Manipulators are a living testament to the truth of Jean Giraualoux's famous comment, "The secret of success is sincerity—once you can fake that, you've got it made."

These kids can be quite mild in family settings. Even so, they generally know a lot more about their rights than their responsibilities. It is important to know that the behavior of Manipulators can vary wildly in different settings.

It is a disappointing moment for a parent to realize that their golden child who mixes well with other adults and acts as sweet as pie can be an absolute dictator when it comes to playing with children his own age.

Try to never leave these kids unsupervised in a group of children, as they will often gang up and play other kids off against one another. This is usually done by siding with one child at the expense of a second.

When these kids fall out with friends, they usually do so in a big way.

They can be quite vehement and can quite purposely leave other people out. As a result, they often need a lot of help to build ongoing peer groups and to learn how to make up and resolve differences with friends.

When conflict with parents occurs, the Manipulators of this world really know how to push all the buttons. They can be quite provocative and accusing, and can tell their parents they are stupid.

Manipulators are children who not only need to be the center of attention, they have to be the best. Getting between one of these kids and their goal means you risk abuse, being put down, and sometime having a verbal brawl that would embarrass most lawyers and even flush the cheeks of a few politicians.

Why they need help

The Manipulators of this world are extremely ambitious and goal-focused. Now you might say that sounds well suited to success in the modern world. The difficulty arises when you realize it is a case of winning or nothing. There is no second best for Manipulators, so unless they win every time (and let's face it, who really does?) they are devastated. Their self-esteem is not based on anything positive.

Essentially they work from the idea that the end justifies the means. If winning (or impressing adults) requires that they lie, cheat, or denigrate others, they will do it. Their moral reasoning can be based on expediency.

Another difficulty facing the Manipulators is that they only connect with a limited range of people. Unless helped to broaden their social skills, they end up at best respected, most often feared, and rarely liked. There is a risk of loneliness.

Common adult responses to misbehavior

Parents often shift in their response to misbehavior. The first response is disbelief—"You must be talking about another child"—as their child has done so well in playing sweet to adults. This is followed by shock as the parents become aware of some of their child's social interactions. This can lead to them trying to find what has caused this change in their child. Generally there hasn't been a change in their child; the only change has been in their own awareness.

The most common response that follows is shame. Parents worry that their child will grow up to be a bully. This is not inevitable, but work needs to be done to help the Manipulators thrive. This response can be followed by a desire to catch them out, which can build a world of distrust and sneakiness.

One of the bizarre features of parenting bright kids is that you can start behaving in the very ways you are trying to help your child not to behave in. For example, a parent who is concerned about their child keeping secrets starts rummaging through her room and diaries without telling her. The great risk is that you role-model the very behavior you want to lessen.

Common responses when told to stop misbehaving

Ever see the scene from *The Exorcist* where Linda Blair's head spins around and green bile floods from her mouth? Well, the response of Manipulators when parents "call them out" on their actions is pretty impressive, but it's not quite as bad as that. They will often lie and then, if that doesn't work, will blame you, your intentions, your intelligence, and even your sanity.

Strategies for parenting Manipulators

As these kids have usually spent many years playing cute to adults, and are supremely skilled at presenting themselves as competent and mature, the first issue confronting their parents is, have they allowed their child too free a rein? These kids may be seriously under-parented and may need increased surveillance to learn how to interact well with their peers.

To really help these kids, a big time investment is required. They are used to being the Little Prince or Princess, and adjusting to having their near-royal status changed takes some time.

These kids begin to change when they finally meet an adult who has got them stitched, someone who has got their number. Manipulators often thrive when they feel their parents have eyes in the back of their heads, as the parents pick up on small behaviors and don't give them an inch.

This doesn't need to be nasty or punitive. In fact, the most effective way is to cheerily say to a Manipulator, "I'm hanging out with you" or "Guess what? You get to come with me today." They may well roll their eyes and complain or protest, "I haven't done anything wrong." To which the best response is to say sweetly, "No, but you might."

What is fascinating to watch is the bond that forms between a Manipulator and a parent who takes on this very proactive style of parenting. There is almost a sense of relief from the child that finally they have encountered a fully fledged, valid adult.

David was 13 years of age and a very skilled Manipulator. His parents had separated years before and David had used the confused communication between his parents to embark on a rather successful life of petty crime.

This all came tumbling down when David was caught with a computer in hand in a local school at 10 p.m. by the police. His parents and teachers were shocked, and told me this was completely out of character. We decided to use the approach of intensive adult contact, and included the school in this. For the next six weeks, David barely had a moment when there wasn't an adult by his side including him, accompanying him, and keeping an eye on him. At first he moaned and grumbled about this, but eventually came to enjoy the adult contact.

Manipulators can be very successful at developing a support network of hangers-on. These might be friends, but they may also be grandparents or brothers or sisters. When you start to help these kids stop their manipulative ways, do it out of sight of the hangers-on.

Helping a Manipulator become a "reciprocator"—that is, someone who can give as well as take—means helping her learn the skills of getting along with others. This is a lesson most Manipulators find difficult to grasp. It's important to remember that reciprocators are usually happier people than Manipulators. The ability to be considerate of other people's needs is an important predictor of life success as well as a source of resilience.

These kids can grow into great leaders and can show great leadership. Let them select the goal, such as making a particular person happy. Address their issues, especially low self-esteem (see Chapter 20). Generally their self-esteem is based on outdoing others rather than on something positive.

Takeaways

Manipulators:
- can wrap adults around their little finger, eat them for breakfast, hoodwink, and charm the socks off them,
- can bully other children,
- are very, very good at playing cute to adults,
- are determined and somewhat single-minded,
- are extremely ambitious and goal-focused,
- when they fall out with friends, it's usually in a big way,
- need to be the center of attention and the best,
- work from the idea that the end justifies the means, and
- will lie and denigrate others to win (or to impress adults).

3

The Negotiators

Motto:

There's always another audience

Mascots

Bart Simpson: with his "eat my shorts" attitude and rapid-fire retorts, Bart is a natural Negotiator.

Emmeline Pankhurst (1858–1928): worked tirelessly for women's rights. Frequently jailed for her militancy, Emmeline would go on a hunger strike, then would eventually be released in order for her to regain her health. She would then be put back in jail, where she would again starve herself.

Dennis the Menace: the card-sharp, wheeling-and-dealing, trouble-making boy of comic-book infamy.

Cleopatra: astutely ruled Egypt from 51–30 BC, using her alliances with Julius Caesar and Mark Antony to bring prosperity and peace to her country.

These kids are as sharp as a tack, wheeler-dealers who can run rings around you if you are not careful. You come up with two options, these kids come up with a third. You have three options, they'll come up with a fourth. There is a long history of these types of characters, from Bart Simpson to Tom Sawyer and Huck Finn—all of whom, if they were in school today, would be likely to be on serious medication.

Characteristics and behaviors

These kids have a strong future career in business. They seem to be born with street smarts in abundance. They are able to engage people and humor them. People like them (mostly). Parenting them is an experience half-filled with humor and half-filled with a desire to throttle them.

> *Golden Rule: Negotiators have more energy to put into any battle than any parent ever has.*

This means it is very important, when parenting these children, to select your negotiation issues carefully. Too many, and not only will you be ineffective, you'll be exhausted as well.

The Negotiators of this world are cunning and funny. They will try to control by resisting direction and requests. They engage other people by being jokesters, and they are generally good at it. It's just that they don't know when to stop.

A common thread with Negotiators is that they use distraction to get out of any area in which they might fail. The truth for these kids is a very flexible commodity that can be shaped to fit almost any circumstance.

There is a great story in which an old guy says to a younger one: "No matter how far you travel, or how smart you get, always remember this: some day, somewhere, a guy is going to come up to you, and show you a nice new pack of cards with an unbroken seal and that guy is going to bet you that the Jack of Spades will jump out of this pack and squirt cider in your ear. But son," the old guy says, "do not bet him, for sure as you do, you are going to get an ear full of cider."

The Negotiator is always the one squirting the cider.

Why they need help

As humorous and engaging as these children are, wheeling and dealing often gives them a bad name with teachers, and they can end up in all sorts of trouble. Also, in their working lives they need to learn about integrity—doing what you say you will, being who you say you are. See Chapter 25 for more on this.

Common adult responses to misbehavior

The funniness of Negotiators can make parents change their responses from laughing with them to feeling used by them. We all run the risk of becoming our own worst enemy with these kids. The reason is because they are funny, really funny. So we laugh along with them in the hope that this will build goodwill. Ha! These kids will turn on you in a matter of moments, and you can easily end up feeling used and personally offended by them.

Just as the parents of Manipulators can easily mirror the very behavior they want to stop by trying to catch their child out, parents of Negotiators also run the risk of trying to outwit them. This results in power struggles, with parents saying things like, "I'll show *them* not to defy me," "I *will* have them submit to my way of doing things," or "They don't respect me."

Common responses when told to stop misbehaving

The Negotiators of this world don't want to show you they are compliant. A dismissive shrug of the shoulder or a wise crack is often all the response you will get.

Some Negotiators will actually change their behavior when requested to do so by parents, but do it in such a "card-sharp" way that it doesn't seem like they have complied. Parents need to focus on actions, not on words or attitude.

Other Negotiators will suddenly find themselves "injured" and "in pain" in an attempt to distract from the issue at hand. Some Negotiators can really enjoy a short burst of ill health.

Strategies for parenting Negotiators

These children can be wonderfully affectionate and, when you get behind the attitude, they are often very sweet. Most of the time, however, they are fiercely independent, and this can leave parents craving touch, hugs, and affection. Parents need to be watchful to ensure that times of affection are not times for negotiation. Don't let them kiss and cuddle you into winning.

The most common issue I see for parents of this type is that they vacillate from one extreme to the other. Moving quickly from a desire to cuddle to a desire to strangle is not good. It's inconsistent and it lets the child run your home. Don't get me wrong, these are wonderful kids—you just don't want them running your life for you.

Parenting these kids can be a tricky business. While you don't want to crush their individuality, they often want to be an exception to any condition you lay down, based on some (possibly entirely fictitious) special need. At times it is necessary to play down their specialness or difference and to emphasize that there are no exceptions to your important rules.

These kids need a bottom line that is clear and unambiguous, and the results of crossing that line must be etched in their memories. For a parent, it's important not to go for too much, too soon. Decide on one or, at most, two important rules and have very clear consequences. Give these kids very clear expectations, lay out the boundaries, then lay out the boundaries again. Tell them there is no negotiation.

Don't fight and don't give in. In moments of conflict, withdraw and calm down. Remember, your aim is not to have them submit to your will, it is to have them develop integrity and a consideration of others' needs, which will help them to thrive in life.

In heated moments, words are your worst enemy. Negotiators are extremely talented at twisting and turning words into humor, provocation, or distraction. Words are home territory for these kids.

Most Negotiators love an audience for their jokes and actions. Battling with them in front of friends or, even worse, extended family members is pointless. Always take them away from the audience before talking with them.

Many of these kids are bedazzled by rewards. A small prize can often be more valued by them than praise, especially if they believe they have beaten the odds to get it. Use tangible rewards such as free time, food, and stickers rather than praise alone.

Jenny was one of the funniest kids I've ever seen in therapy. By the age of eight, she had both of her parents eating from the palm of her hand. She was a card-sharp, lightning-fast-witted Bart Simpson, and it won't surprise me when one day she is an exceptionally successful businesswoman.

Jenny was also an accomplished escapologist. She could disappear from school, find her way home, and spend hours on the computer. When the school called Jenny's parents to start the search party, a soap opera unfolded. Adults rushed frantically in all directions trying to find her.

Jenny's exasperated parents would then spend hours forcefully explain to her the importance of school and the need to let people know where you are, as well as safety issues. All sensible issues to discuss. They would then extract a solemn vow from Jenny that she would never disappear from school again.

After a few days of school attendance, guess where Jenny was? You got it in one! On a school day, she was at home in front of her beloved computer.

Her parents came along fuming. "She promises me she'll never run away from school again and then she does exactly the opposite," her mother groaned.

When I saw Jenny alone and asked whether she meant to upset her parents, her eyes sparkled and she grinned cheekily.

The first change was for her parents to learn to stop extracting meaningless promises and to instead focus on Jenny's actions. We agreed that for every time Jenny disappeared from school she would lose access to the computer for two days. Over the next six weeks, Jenny tested this out several times before learning that her parents were not going to spend hours discussing the matter: they just disabled the computer and got on with their lives.

After a few dramatic episodes, Jenny realized that she wasn't getting the usual response, and decided that losing two days of computer game time simply wasn't worth it.

Takeaways

Negotiators:

- are as sharp as a tack—wheelers and dealers who can run rings around you if you are not careful,
- always have another option,
- are cunning, conning, and funny,
- control by resisting direction and requests,
- engage other people by being jokesters, and are generally good at it, but they don't know when to stop,
- use distraction to avoid any area in which they might fail,
- see truth as a very flexible commodity,
- don't want to show they are compliant—a dismissive shrug or a wise-crack is often all the response you will get,
- are fiercely independent, and
- can twist words into humor, provocation, or distraction.

4

The Debaters

Motto:

Whoever has the last word, wins!

Mascots

Margaret Thatcher: aka "The Iron Lady" (a nickname she embraced), Britain's first female prime minister had a formidable will and zero self-doubt. "Thatcherism," with its industry privatizations, has changed the world.

Germaine Greer: author of the landmark 1970 book, *The Female Eunuch*, about women's liberation, she has been arguing with everyone ever since.

John F. Kennedy: the youngest-ever U.S. president and a compelling orator who persuaded Soviet leader Nikita Khruschev to withdraw the missiles during the Cuban missile crisis.

Jerry Springer: loud-mouthed talk-show host famous for getting his guests to physically attack each other. A born "contrarian."

The Australian journalist George Negus once interviewed the then British Prime Minister, Margaret Thatcher, and suggested to her that some people didn't like her policies. Mrs. Thatcher looked affronted, and responded by asking him to name those people. That is why she is such a wonderful mascot for these children.

If you ask one of these children to tidy their bedroom, they will look at you in an affronted, flabbergasted sort of way and then ask, "Why me?"

The Debaters of this world, be they male or female, are the economic rationalists of the emotional world. They will hold you to account.

Characteristics and behaviors

The Debaters' theme song should be, "What about me?" Common statements you will hear from these kids include:

"You never let me do that when I was his age."

"But she got ..."

"It's not my turn."

"Her present was bigger."

"It's not fair."

"I did it last time."

"I didn't get as large a piece of cake."

"I didn't get as much time on ...."

These kids watch out so keenly for the fairness and balance of rights and wrongs, you feel like you have a Human Rights Commissioner living in your home. They seem destined for success in fields of law, equity, and justice. They are very determined and very verbal children who can use language well—a deadly combination!

Why they need help

Debaters are remarkable children and adults. Energetic to the point of being driven, they won't let up on you for a moment. While they have incredible strengths, they need to learn a variety of ways of interacting in the world.

Unfortunately, these kids are often not tuned in to their own emotions. They are aware of resentment and a lack of fairness, but that disguises insecurity about whether they are good enough and lovable enough. Unless we help them to feel secure and to broaden their ways of dealing with people, they are on their way to having a chip on their shoulder, which they will deal with by controlling others.

Common adult responses to misbehavior

Usually parents try to reason with Debaters and explain at length why it *is* fair and why the Debater shouldn't feel aggrieved. No one wants to be seen as unfair. But almost always this is a complete waste of time. Every parent of a Debater will do this from time to time, though, as a matter of form.

When your reasonable explanations of fairness fail to win the day, parents often experience exasperation and frustration. This often leads to parents reducing the amount of time they spend with the kids in the hope this will reduce the amount of conflict, or else using more words to try to justify their actions. The parent's and the child's behavior thus starts to mirror one another—neither feels understood, and an uneasy cold war breaks out.

Common responses when told to stop misbehaving

Have you ever watched politicians debating? Have you ever heard a politician from one side say to the opposing party, "Yes, I can see you're right. You have convinced me"? I thought not.

These kids won't be convinced either. The word that comes to mind is "indignant."

Strategies for parenting Debaters

These are very verbal children who can tie you up in never-ending debates about who got the most and was it fair. While sometimes you will feel the need to debate, if only to defend your own decision making, it is, sadly, often a pointless exercise.

Mrs. McIngle told me that her son was always complaining about being overlooked. His brothers, he said, were loved more, were driven more places, and got bigger presents than he did.

"Of course," said Mrs. McIngle, "what parent wouldn't worry about this? I tried to discuss the relative merits: 'Remember when I bought you the bike? Remember when we had lunch out together?'

"None of this impressed him at all. I started taking him out shopping, which worked for a while, but then he wanted bigger and bigger presents. My income couldn't keep up with his buying habits. Also, I started to feel guilty again. The others were missing out. Finally I realized it wasn't shopping and gifts he needed."

Don't debate these children for long periods; instead, respond with affection. For example, "You poor dear, you must be so unhappy to be feeling that way, let me give you a hug." Deal with their hurt feelings. Offer understanding rather than pity, then set up opportunities for success.

Setting aside some special time with these children each week that is child-directed is particularly valuable. (This is a good idea with all kids, but is really helpful with Debaters.)

Some Debaters need to have structured times, e.g., start at..., finish at .... Then they can know that this time belongs to them, and they don't have to struggle or complain to maintain your attention.

One-on-one time often works best to begin with. These children have learned that one way to get affection and attention is through disputes. This takes a while to undo. Where possible, praise them in private. Nonverbal signs such as ruffling their hair or patting their shoulder also work well as reminders that they are loved.

Families with Debaters need to have consistency and structure, as a freewheeling lifestyle quickly descends into a debate about fairness. Unless you are prepared to go to the International Court of Dispute Resolution every time you want to do something with your kids, put routines into family life and ensure that everyone gets a fair go.

Debaters often battle with their brothers or sisters. These skirmishes can become so intense they can make life miserable for everyone.

If my earlier political example didn't make this clear enough, Debaters are masters of emotionally accusing others, e.g., "He did it," "It was her fault," and "You always take her side." They don't have the shifty subtlety of a Manipulator; they go at you with the determination of a hung-over, disgruntled pit-bull terrier with a terrible case of piles.

These kids often seem to be blessed with great memories, which they use to source examples to back their case. Let's look in on a typical conversation:

Parent: *John, it's four o'clock, could you please feed the dog?*
John: *It's not my turn, Elizabeth has to do it. I fed her guinea pig last Thursday.*
Parent: *[repeating] John, it's four o'clock, could you please feed the dog?*
John: *You always pick on me. It's not fair.*
Parent: *No I don't, now go and feed the dog.*
John: *Yes you do! How about the time you took her to the movies and I had to do homework?*
Parent: *That's because you had work overdue.*
John: *You love her more than me. You always have!*

At this rate, the dog could well starve to death in this household because John will never voluntarily bring the discussion back to doing his chore.

If allowed to, Debaters can spend enormous amounts of time accusing and blaming others until it becomes a habit. Either walk away, saying, "I can't listen to this right now," or look at them sadly and say, "I can see you must be feeling very sad in order to be saying those things. Come and have a hug."

Takeaways

Debaters:
- are very determined,
- have a strong sense of fairness and right and wrong,
- always argue the point,
- are very verbal—they can use language well,
- are energetic to the point of being driven,
- are often not tuned in to their own emotions,
- are aware of resentment and a lack of fairness, which often disguises an insecurity about whether they are good enough and lovable enough, and
- can be indignant.

5

The Competitors

Motto:

Fight to
the death

Mascots

Winston Churchill: the English statesman who successfully led Britain through World War Two. He was an indomitable, victory-at-any-cost Competitor.

Lance Armstrong: the record seven-time winner of what is considered the world's toughest sporting event, cycling's Tour de France.

Alexander the Great: single-handedly changed the ancient world in about 10 years. Incredibly, he led his army to victories in Asia Minor, Syria, and Egypt without incurring a single defeat. He conquered and linked the area from Greece in the west, north to the Danube, south into Egypt, and as far east as India.

Martina Navratilova: the peerless tennis player who, in her day, was a regular winner of the Wimbledon singles and doubles events.

> *"I'll fight you in the kitchen, I'll fight you in the bathroom,*
> *I'll fight you anywhere."*

Remind you of anyone? Yes, it's little Winston. Welcome to his world.

Characteristics and behaviors

These children have incredible spirit. They could conquer the world. They will certainly try to conquer your home. The battle can rage on and off for years, leaving you with a sense that never before have so few battled for so long, for so little.

Children with the Winston Churchill syndrome are most likely well suited to future careers in sales, politics, or law. Every interaction has the potential to be a source for battle.

These kids like to boast, and they can't bear to lose. Coming second is tantamount to complete failure for them. In a dispute, these kids don't just dig their heels in—they dig their whole bodies in as well. They are defiant in the extreme, and the expression "Cut off their nose to spite their face" is tailor-made for these kids. Their need to win at any cost means they will disregard the consequences of their actions.

Why they need help

When winning is everything, life becomes scary. These children can be world-beaters but they can also be lonely and, while they would never show this publicly, can be fearful and have quite low self-esteem. When winning is everything, you fear loss.

> *"The moment of victory is much too short to live for that and for nothing else."*
>
> Martina Navratilova

Competitors are often sponges for attention, and rely on it. Think about why they need so much attention and try to lessen their constant need for it.

Common adult responses to misbehavior

The risk in dealing with the Competitors of the child world is that parents enter a power battle. This not only invariably fails (at best, you get compliance, submission, and resentment), it also consolidates the child's view that the world is "either do to first or be done to."

Having a power battle with these kids is like entering the arms race. Parents need to be much, much cleverer than that.

Common responses when told to stop misbehaving

These kids are indomitable and defiant, and will do anything rather than lose face. They will pretend not to care. They will argue and persist. They will continue the behavior even when it goes against their interests because they are so entrenched in the need to win.

Strategies for parenting Competitors

The first thing to realize is that consequences make no difference. You tell a Competitor that she is grounded and she'll dig her heels in, look you straight in the eye, and say, "I don't care, ground me for as long as you like, I'm happy in my room." Tell her her allowance is docked and she'll tell you she didn't need it anyway. Tell her television is banned for a week, and she'll tell you there's nothing worth watching this week anyway.

Often I hear parents pleading with Competitors along the lines of, "If you'd just do what we want, then you could come out of your room" or "If you'd just feed the cat [or whatever task the debate is about] then you'd get pocket money." Ha! Don't die waiting, because that's how long it will take. These kids are determined, obstinate, and fiercely self-willed.

Don't ever enter into conflict with these children in front of their peers. You will be bound to come off second best. In fact, getting into a stand-off position with these kids is never, ever going to work. I know it sounds sneaky, but you've got to play to your own strengths and prey upon their vulnerabilities.

Competitors often respond well when parents challenge them. It is best to use third-person challenges rather than the "I bet you can't ..." variety, as you don't want to give the impression of being a doubting parent. If, for example, you wanted a budding Martina to clean up her clothes or take charge of her homework, some types of challenges would be:

"Not many people would believe you could ..."

"Not many people would believe you were old enough to ..."

"Not many people would believe you were responsible enough to ..."

"Most parents wouldn't allow someone your age to ...."

Eventually these challenges can be extended into "Personal Bests." Rather than comparing their performance with others, it can be preferable to have them compare their current performance with past outcomes. For example, parents can develop this by asking questions like, "If you had to give yourself a score out of 10 for how well you rode a bike [or any activity] a year ago, what would you say? And what score would you give yourself now?"

The concern parents often express in regard to Competitors is not only how to guide them, but also how to help them cope with not winning all the time. If you fear losing, it means that you often avoid trying new activities you may not do well at.

This often leads to a puzzling dilemma for parents: they know their child is passionately motivated, but at school barely lifts a finger to try anything new. We'll discuss this more later, but it is important to keep your Winston trying different activities.

Comments like "I'm no good at English" or "I suck at Math" are important to ban, as they can operate as powerful cop-outs for Competitors. Say something like, "Remember, this is a no-put-down house, and that includes no put-downs of yourself. Anyway, nobody will believe you."

Winning comes naturally to these kids. Playing games doesn't. Look around for opportunities to involve them in activities that don't have a winner and a loser: theater sports, drama, Frisbee throwing, kite flying, exercise. You may also need to teach them how to win gracefully rather than gloating and boasting.

Competitors are also generally good at taking on responsibilities. So making sure they have a few age-appropriate areas of responsibility helps them to develop.

Takeaways

Competitors:
- are defiant in the extreme,
- must win at any cost,
- boast,
- can be world-beaters, but can also need attention,
- treat a power struggle like it's the arms race,
- are indomitable—they will do anything rather than lose face,
- will pretend not to care, and
- will continue their behavior even when it goes against their interests because they are so entrenched in the need to win.

6

The Dare Devils

Motto:

No fear

Mascots

Steve Irwin: the late "Crocodile Hunter" is a great example of a thrill-seeking Dare Devil—he did wonderful conservation work with the world's most dangerous animals.

Harry Houdini: the thrilling magician who amazed audiences with his daring escape attempts. His most famous act involved being suspended upside-down in a locked glass-and-steel cabinet full of water—and then getting out alive.

"Evel" Knievel: the late stuntman best known for his public displays of long-distance, high-altitude motorbike tricks.

Marco Polo: the daring fourteenth-century adventurer who traveled from Europe as far as China, well beyond the limits of the known world.

A friend of mine works every year at the local State Fair. Now, if you are like me and only go to this type of event every so often, there is something you have probably noticed: from time to time an announcement will come over the loudspeaker, "Would the parents of Harvey Brown or Sally Boyston please collect your child from Lost and Found?"

According to my friend, it is the same kids who show up time and time again at Lost and Found. At first she thought the parents of these children were neglectful or careless, and then she realized they all had similar charac-teristics: they were Dare Devils. They belong to the Steve Irwin club. They are forceful and exciting chil-dren to parent! In fact, parenting them is often an extreme sport in itself!

Characteristics and behaviors

About 15 percent of children are fearless, with little regard for their own safety or the safety of those around them. Don't worry, this is not a product of your parenting style—it seems they are born that way.

These kids are high sensation-seekers and they love a challenge, thrills, and excitement. These people often do well long-term in careers that give them an outlet for their daring nature, such as emergency services workers—firefighters, ambulance officers, emergency room nurses, police officers, stunt people, and extreme sports participants.

You can pick these kids. They often have limps, bandages, or plaster casts! Their parents are often seen filling out insurance forms.

They are not usually gifted in the art of forward planning. You will rarely if ever hear one of them say, "Hang on a minute, I'm just going to pop over and see how far I can slide down that banister." No, these are impulsive children—they just do it. As a result, disappearances from home, getting lost in shopping malls, and scrapes and cuts and bruises are common events in their lives.

They are often very sweet-natured people whose intent is not to worry or alarm you. In fact, as they experience little fear themselves, the thought that you might be alarmed doesn't even enter their heads.

One mother described a trip to the local fairground with her Dare Devil: "At one point in the afternoon, the Ferris wheel stopped as people looked anxiously upwards at a child standing and swinging out from his seat. As I looked up, a sense of familiarity crept over me …."

Why they need help

The Dare Devils of this world try out things that make the rest of us tremble in fear. I suspect that many explorers of the past, Walter Raleigh, Christopher Columbus, Isabelle Eberhardt, James Cook, Vasco de Gama, and David Livingstone, all had a healthy dose of Dare Devildom. It allowed them to go where few others would.

Parenting these children combines admiration and fear for their survival. Becoming immune to the censuring looks of other parents can also be a useful talent to develop when parenting a Dare Devil.

Dare Devils need help in staying as safe as possible. They are not good at assessing risks and deciding not to do things. They need adults who are prepared to say things like, "No way are you climbing that tree, you are staying right here!"

Common adult responses to misbehavior

Frustration and exasperation are common responses to these kids' exploits. This comes out of fear. One father told me he spent more time in medical rooms than at his own work, and then turned to his son and said, "There we were, back in the doctor's waiting room, all because you had to see what would happen if you tried a triple backward-spin off the diving board!"

It's not just boys that do this. Girls can also involve themselves in risky ventures, either physically or socially.

Throwing a protective blanket over your child can be tempting ... and, unfortunately, disastrous. These kids need to immerse themselves in life so they can learn to make wise judgments and decisions. Sure, they may have a worried parent nearby to help them avoid too many diabolical outcomes, but they will need to take *some* risks.

Common responses when told to stop misbehaving

Their most common response is to be perplexed and mystified: "What are you worrying about?," these kids will ask. Dare Devils are optimistic—so optimistic that they overestimate their own abilities:

"Sure, I can jump off a wall that high and still land safely on my feet."

"Sure, I'll be fine walking home alone after the party."

"Next time I'll know to roll when I land."

Strategies for parenting Dare Devils

You are not going to wean these kids away from the thrills and the spills. Instead, we need to find positive forms of risk taking: camping, motocross, bungee jumping, video games, paintball, other extreme sports, and visual/drama activities.

Even with positive forms of risk taking, there is one absolutely essential piece of advice: get good medical coverage!

Calming down their environment is essential. These kids do have calm times, but only when things around them are calm. Chapter 13, on mood changing, applies especially to Dare Devils. Use lighting, music, movement, and food as your allies.

In moments of conflict with Dare Devils it is necessary to remove any audience of peers before trying to resolve an issue. These kids have a reputation to uphold as the wildest, coolest, freakiest kid around. Far better to say, "Can I have a word for a moment?," and take them away from their audience of peers than having a ding-dong battle that gets nowhere.

The love these kids have for intensity means they don't think things through. Many of them have difficulty getting things in the right order. Help them to develop the skill of sequencing by asking lots of questions when they are planning something:

"So tell me what the first thing you will do is …"

"And what happens next?"

"And then what happens?"

Getting them to talk through the steps may be a little like pulling teeth, but it helps them prepare for their risks a bit better. Also, relaxation, mental imagery, visualization, and concentration exercises can help them train to become more focused.

It is wise to develop a code of clear nonverbal signals with this child. For example: "If you hear this whistling sound, it

"IF I SPIN FAST ENOUGH WILL THE CAT AND I MAKE IT INTO OUTER SPACE?"

means I need you to come to me right away," or, "If you see me on the beach with one hand raised over my head, that means you have swum too far out to sea."

Mr. Noble's son was nicknamed "Leaping Leo" by the kids at school. Leaping Leo was a legend, not only in his own school but also in the surrounding towns. According to the rumors that served as Leo's personal public relations kit, Leo had leapt from the roof of one school building to another on more than one occasion. Mr. Noble was alarmed. It was true that Leo had been involved in a jumping incident, but over a very short distance.

By the time this leap had gone the rounds of the rumor-mongers, Leo was almost at Olympic long-jump status. The trouble was, Leo was beginning to believe his own press.

"We are worried," explained Mr. Noble, "that if Leo is pressured into leaping, he might seriously damage himself."

That night we talked to Leo and told him that every good sportsperson needs training. We took him for long-jump training and insisted that before he even contemplated a leap, we needed to have at least 24 hours' notice. This way we get advance warning and can channel his energies into other areas.

Takeaways

Dare Devils:
- are high sensation-seekers who love a challenge and thrills,
- often have limps, bandages, or plaster casts,
- are not usually gifted in the art of forward planning,
- may disappear from home and get lost a lot,
- are sweet natured,
- are fearless—they try things that make the rest of us tremble,
- are not good at assessing risks,
- are not good at deciding not to do things, and
- are so optimistic that they overestimate their own abilities.

7

The Passive Resisters

Motto:

"Problem?
What problem?"

Mascots

Mahatma Gandhi: led India to independence from British rule through his process of passive resistance, thereby raising the habit of doing nothing to an art form. During his political career, he developed *satyagraha* ("devotion to truth"), a new nonviolent way to redress wrongs.

Aung San Suu Kyi: Burma's long-suffering pro-democracy leader and a noted prisoner of conscience, she was awarded the Nobel Peace Prize for her nonviolent struggle under a repressive dictatorship.

Characteristics and behaviors

Passive Resisters are vague, secretive, and disorganized. Some of them move through life slowly, resembling the characters from the children's television show *The Thunderbirds*.

These are the kids that will look at you blankly when asked something. For example, if you were to say something like, "Why didn't you hand your homework in?," they would likely reply, "Homework? What homework? Nobody asked me to do any homework."

These kids are as cool as a cucumber; their parents are the ones who feel infuriated and blocked out. One of these kids reflected recently on his upbringing by saying, "I had a wonderful childhood, it's just that it nearly sent my parents mad."

Passive Resisters are sometimes very bright and very sensitive people. They can retreat and avoid life in order to avoid failure. They are similar to Competitors in that they don't care much about consequences.

These kids almost have a style of learned helplessness in which passivity, ducking their head, and hoping it will all go away seem to be their main life strategies. They often like to fly under the radar, and seem to live on the periphery of the main arena of life.

Increasingly, I hear parents talking about this group in their late teens and early twenties, as they hover around home avoiding the main challenges of life—to the great frustration of their parents. Where there has been a separation or family break-up, these behaviors become accentuated.

These kids are so calm on the outside, you could think they are implacable. They often retreat from life and are very private about their thoughts and feelings. They can seem to be out of touch with their surroundings. They often lose possessions and appear not to listen or take information in. They can be hard to get going.

If you have a child who resembles this group of behaviors, congratulations, you have a potential powerhouse on your hands.

The parents, who become alternately perplexed and infuriated with their child's behavior, find themselves saying imploringly, "Just talk to me, tell me what's going on." When communication is this frustrating, you may need to send in the interrogation team!

Why they need help

Passive Resisters are very good at isolating themselves, spending endless hours in their bedroom reading, playing video games, and generally avoiding human interaction. Being happy in your own company is one thing; being in withdrawal is quite something else.

It is often difficult to gauge the level of concern we should have for these young people, partly because it is so difficult to engage them in a discussion about their thoughts or feelings.

A typical discussion goes something like:

> **Parent:** *"How are you?"*
> **Child:** *"All right" [or "Not bad"].*
> **Parent:** *"Anything special happen today?"*
> **Child:** *"Nope."*
> **Parent:** *"What would you like for dinner?"*
> **Child:** *"Whatever you're cooking."*

By this stage, most sane parents will be gnashing their teeth! They know that for their child to thrive in the world, she has to learn to communicate, empathize, and connect with other human beings.

Common adult responses to misbehavior

The great temptation for parents of Passive Resisters is to want to rev them up, motivate them, get them inspired and switched on. Parents can also start pleading with them, "Just tell me what you want."

When these attempts to get inside their heads or to get them moving don't work, parents are left worrying even more. This then sets in motion a cycle of concern alternating with fury.

Common responses when told to stop misbehaving

Passive Resisters are minimalists. They are often placid and noncommittal. Communication can boil down to "What?," "Dunno," "As if …," and "Whatever."

Strategies for parenting Passive Resisters

If these characteristics describe your child, it is time to start bringing him back into the emotional world of other people. Several things don't work:

- yelling, insisting, pleading, or appealing to his better nature,
- trying to be a motivational coach, and
- trying to guess what he is thinking by filling in his silences with your own words.

As stated, some of these children and young people are very bright and highly sensitive. Some of them also have strong moral values. One strategy parents often tell me works is to increase their responsibilities.

There is a time in many children's lives when they would prefer to "grow down" rather than grow up. At this time, both boys and girls will go back and play with toys that they have not played with for years. This can be anxiety-provoking for parents, who may worry that their child has been traumatized. Generally, of course, this is not the case. Instead, their child is re-capturing his childhood memories through this form of play.

The behavior of many Passive Resisters is an amplification of this tendency. They retreat to a world of privacy. The temptation with them is to try to cajole, persuade, or entice them out of this state. This rarely works.

Set out to give yourself several months of relationship building. During this time, try to remain calm. Speak to them directly and look them in the eye at the same time. Don't take vague shrugs as an answer—"Dunno" is not a word you will understand. Decrease pressure and increase presence. Make it very clear to them that it is not an option to avoid some family interactions.

Passive Resisters are often good at caring for pets and younger children. Look for opportunities where they can build their confidence and competence by caring for others.

> *Mrs. Chin's daughter retired to her bedroom. "It was like she was on strike," said Mrs. Chin. "At first we let it go. She said she was tired, had a lot of homework. I was worried she might be stressed or depressed. She didn't seem her usual self, but told me not to worry. Finally I got angry and told her she must come down for dinner. She wouldn't. One night I lost it. I said if she won't come down for dinner, we'll all go up. The family ate every evening meal for three weeks in her bedroom. After a while we stopped taking the plates back to the kitchen afterwards. Eventually she gave in. At least now we get to see her at meal times. I'm now working on having her talk at meal times!"*

Takeaways

Passive Resisters:
- are secretive and private about their thoughts and feelings,
- can seem out of touch with their surroundings,
- often lose possessions and appear not to listen or take in information,
- can be hard to get going,
- isolate themselves,
- spend endless hours in their bedroom reading, and generally avoid human interaction,
- are difficult to engage in a discussion about their thoughts or feelings,
- are minimalists, and
- are placid and non-committal—communication can boil down to "What?," "Dunno," "As if ...," and "Whatever."

Yikes—my kid is all of the above!

If you think your child can wield the influence of a Henry Kissinger, be as cheeky as Bart Simpson, dispute a point with the aplomb of Margaret Thatcher, show the competitiveness of Winston Churchill with a blast of Dare Devil combined with a smidgin of Gandhi's passive resistance—don't despair. Initially, many bright kids appear to be a bit of everything.

These ways of behaving are things all children engage in to some extent. Any child can do the odd Angelica or the occasional Bart. The risk for bright kids is that they can lock into a routine that is not really helpful to them.

Parents often report that it takes a bit of time to properly learn their child's style. They then use this knowledge to form a relationship that helps their child to broaden out as a person and to have more choices about ways of relating.

In the end, accurately identifying your child's type is not as important as starting to think in new ways about helping her to play to her strengths. Be prepared to experiment for a while.

Part Two

THE DEVELOPMENTAL STAGES OF BRIGHT KIDS

In the torrid world of parenting bright kids, it is very easy to lose sight of the big picture as you deal with the latest skirmish, insult, or confrontation. This can make parents vulnerable to despair as they lose perspective regarding whether they are raising their bright kid well.

Part Two offers a reminder of the main stages of child development as they relate to bright kids. It is useful to be aware of these stages because this helps us to keep in mind what we should and shouldn't be expecting of these kids at various ages.

8

Infancy and preschool

It's a rocky road, this parenting business. Most parents of bright children start by asking, "What's normal?" This chapter tries to give you a rough guide to this.

Before trying to tackle this question, it is important to remind you that kids develop at different rates. It is always anxiety-provoking for a parent to look at their little Jimmy, who is struggling to work out which end of the pacifier to stick in his mouth, when the neighbor's little genius, Henrietta, has already knocked over *War and Peace* and is currently composing *What Hamlet Did Next*. Nevertheless, remember that children differ: they develop in their own time, and the person who develops fastest is not always the most successful or the cleverest.

Let's repeat that: *the child who develops fastest is not always the most successful or the cleverest.*

As someone once wisely observed, if you turn life into a rat race, whether you win or lose, you always wind up being a rat.

Infancy

We have probably learned more in the past few years about the way people learn and develop than we have in the previous 50 years. Much of this upsurge has been due to the proliferation of positron emission tomography (PET) scan studies.

The squishy blob of grey matter that sits on the top of your neck is the most complex, adaptable, regenerating object we know of. And it's busiest when we are children.

The way the mind develops is not a neat sequence of events. Recent research is confirming what two of the great thinkers of child development (Jean Piaget and Maria Montessori) postulated: that children's minds develop in fits and starts followed by periods of consolidation. These processes were labelled "assimilation" and "accommodation" by Piaget, and were described as "cycles of learning" by Montessori.

In terms of brain development, there appear to be times of overproduction or exuberance during which we may be highly receptive to new information and able to gain specific skills more easily. During childhood and adolescence, this seems to be the way the brain develops—overdoing it in terms of production and then cutting back on what is not needed later. It's a pretty nifty system because it's precisely that overproduction that allows us to choose, to hone and to specialize our skills.

If we map the key social competencies at different ages, we get a rough timeline that can help parents to be aware of priorities.

Development timeline		
Age	**What's happening**	
Birth	Intrigued by difference, especially faces, corners, and stripes	Play is experimentation

Of course there is individual variability as well as gender differences, but nevertheless timelines such as the ones in this chapter can be used to help parents target specific behaviors and learning processes at different times.

Children's brains are much busier and quite a bit cleverer than adults' are. From birth, the brain is busy setting up connections. At birth, each brain cell or neuron has about 2,500 connections called synapses; the number then increases rapidly, so that by two to three years of age there are 15,000 synapses for each neuron. Preschool children have brains that are more active, more connected, and more flexible than ours. In many ways you could argue that you will never be cleverer, more flexible, or more adaptable than you were when you were three.

Up until the age of three, children are like sponges. Given sufficient time and attachment with a caring adult and a reasonably interesting environment, they just learn. They absorb their surroundings and are especially interested in differences. In fact they learn by being attuned to differences. This remains true for all of us throughout our lives.

This means that from birth we are intensely interested in our social environment: we notice difference, we focus our learning towards emotions, we try to draw causal connections between events, and we want to create meaning and try out our knowledge in new settings.

We are born to learn about new places and people and to adjust to what we find there. This means that children already know a whole lot more about learning than adults do.

Much of our sense of belonging and security is laid down in these early years. Basic attitudes—including whether the world is a safe, friendly place or a hostile jungle—are put into place.

Development timeline

Age	What's happening	
First year	Comfort when distressed helps you learn the world is a friendly place	Rapid synaptic brain development

There are many places of power in the world—the Pentagon, Mecca, the Vatican, the Kremlin—but the most powerful of all is the family home. The family is the most powerful structure of human belonging in the world: it is the place where gifts are received, gifts that take a lifetime to unwrap.

If your bright child did not have the calmest, warmest, happiest infancy, don't despair. It doesn't mean she will spend the rest of her days viewing the world as an awful place. It does mean, however, that you may have some work to do to give her more positive ways to live.

Development timeline		
Age	What's happening	
One–two	Parents give children the words through which to live their lives	Play is mainly individual

Preschool stage

Then, at about the age of three or four, something happens and it all changes. It is almost as if four-year-olds stop in their tracks, look around in bewilderment, and express this puzzlement by asking, "Why?"

It is estimated that a four-year-old asks a "why" question every two-and-a-half minutes! All that learning that was happening almost automatically suddenly requires effort.

These are the willful years in which children learn to share, delay gratification, calm themselves down, and develop impulse control. Children who do not learn these skills at this time can learn how to control their impulses later, but it is harder.

Some of you will know adults who never really learned much about impulse control either. You know, those so-called friends of yours who cut a swathe through any social settings, acting in ways that disregard the needs of others, failing to take on responsibility.

Development timeline		
Age	**What's happening**	
Three	Speech develops rapidly Master or Mistress of the Universe (self-absorbed)	Fine and gross motor skills develop
Four	Inquisitive "why" questions Fantasy develops— imagination and fears, including night terrors	Impulse control (self- calming skills)

During these years, children often feel as if they are Masters or Mistresses of the Universe. This means they can feel responsible for things they in reality had no influence over (e.g., upset parents, a poor month financially, a pet's ill health). Considerable time and effort needs to be put into explaining to them why events happen.

This "Master or Mistress of the Universe" feeling also means their tantrums assume great power. It is not a great thing to win every argument when you are three or four years old. Not only does that mean that your tantrums are more powerful than your parents, it also raises the frightening prospect that there is no one stronger to protect you. For parents, this means that you can't afford to crumple every time your child raises his voice. Do not give in to his every last whim.

There are some different priorities in parenting boys and girls at this time. Boys need to be helped to develop fine motor skills. Construction tasks, Lego, games and toys that involve twisting and turning all help boys build the skills that will eventually help them to write well. As the "fight/flight" response is stronger in boys (see Chapter 11), they often need help in containing their anger or tendency to run away if upset. This means applying the strong and compassionate parenting of "fierce friendship."

Girls often need assistance to develop their gross motor skills and to coordinate their large muscle groups. Physical play, ball throwing and catching are helpful, as are games like Twister and musical chairs. Allowing little girls to get dirty is also beneficial. It always seems that the girls who are too ladylike too early are at risk of becoming perfectionists.

Takeaways

- The child who develops fastest is not always the most successful or the cleverest in the long term.
- Children learn in two main ways: imitation, and noticing differences and working out what they mean.
- Our life-long sense of belonging and security is created during this early stage.

9

Early to mid-primary school

"The real menace in dealing with a five-year-old is that in no time at all you begin to sound like a five-year-old."

Jean Kerr

Early primary school

Around the age of six, there is a second surge as the brain starts to use language in increasingly complex ways. The human brain attains 90 percent of its adult weight between four and eight years of age.

Aggression management is important at this time. Entering school every year are children with existing attachment and aggression problems, and they don't just grow out of these, they get worse—much worse! Girls exhibiting these problems at this age do worse long term than boys. For this reason, helping children to learn to avoid the triggers for anger and to not act inappropriately as a result of anger is really important.

Early primary school is a time of forming a peer group. Friendships may not always be based on deep, abiding similarities but nevertheless they can be loyal and emotionally intense attachments. Children may develop a "very best special friend," and may experience grief if a special friend changes social groups or moves out of the area. Try to help your child have a few different playmates and keep building a sense of belonging to family.

The Passive Resisters' withdrawal

Passive Resisters who don't settle into school can show this by separation anxiety or by being extremely quiet. Watch out for these early warning signs and discuss with teachers strategies for engaging them and giving them a sense of success.

Development timeline

Age	What's happening	
Five and six	Wide variation in development at this time	Moral reasoning still forming—will tell lies that are clearly untrue

Anxieties and worries can also invade children's lives. With their developing independence can come anxieties about dangers, death, and injury. Sometimes children will become reluctant to go to school.

Many bright children at this time decide that they are no good at school and say things like, "I'm no good at…" or "I suck at…." Anxiety about their abilities can lead children to give up. It is very important to build positive attitudes about their abilities at this age.

It is difficult to love yourself if you are not first loved. The way we are loved early on forms a stamp on us that is as individual and unique as our fingerprints. It forms the way we react to life and the way we consider death. For many people, this fingerprint of love or abandonment shows up most vividly at times of ritual and gathering—Christmas, birthdays, Easter. This is why we often see conflicts and disappointments resurface at times that represent family closeness and love. The approach we take to major rituals and celebrations tells us much about ourselves.

Mid-primary school

Middle childhood is a time of what is called "latency," when everything lies dormant and settled. Theoretically, it is a time of calm before the storm of puberty. Many parents of teenagers wistfully recall the happy eight-year-old they once had.

One interesting aspect of these years is the "I'm not going to be your friend any more" stage, in which the child begins to exert her willpower in social situations. Many parents find themselves being told on occasions that they are hated by their children. One mother developed a "hate-ometer," in which she kept a count of the number of times she was told she was hated each day—the record was 87 times! One way to look at this is that it prepares you to have a thick skin for later on, when the battles can get really serious. One possible response to a child who insists that they hate you is to say, "You can hate me all you like and *I* can love you just as much as I like."

Negotiator alert!

Early to mid-primary school (about Years 3 and 4) is the time that many Barts decide school success is unachievable for them and take on the job of class clown. Help them to be academically successful by keeping them interested in books through reading to them, in games through playing with them, and in learning by focusing on areas of their interest.

Development timeline

Age	What's happening	
Seven and eight	Listening when other people talk Awareness of the difference between right and wrong	Communicating ideas Wanting to solve problems Using imagination

Sometimes bright children will also be defiant, and will threaten to kill themselves if you don't let them do what they want to do. It's always alarming to hear a child angrily say, "I wish I was dead" or "I didn't ask to be born." While we always need to be watchful for signs of depression, mostly this is defiance rather than depression. Nevertheless, we don't want children to get into a habit of threatening self-harm in order to get their own way. Say, "I can hear you are angry right now and I'm not going to let you hurt yourself."

This is the time to be clear about family rules and expectations. Taking the time to calmly explain rules that help to create the sort of family you want to be is useful. It won't stop them from disputing some of these rules later on, but it does help to have clear, consistent, and calm parenting with reasonably high expectations of the contribution children and young people can make towards family life.

Having high expectations, hopes, and dreams of children and supporting them to contribute positively to family life is one way of promoting resilience in young people. Going on a "treasure hunt" with children—i.e., searching for their talents, skills, and abilities, finding them, and making much of them—assists them to gain positive self-esteem.

Helping boys to develop the ability to put their thoughts into words is important at this time. Involving boys in conversations in which they are not allowed to get away with monosyllabic, caveman-like grunts is important here, and can set them up as good communicators for the remainder of their lives.

Hearing stories or audiobooks (i.e., without any pictures) is a way of helping boys to develop the internal images that help them to build language expression. But I'm not for a moment suggesting that you do away with picture books.

Keeping girls confident with numbers can be useful at this time. Teaching them through the use of money—counting change, working out how much to pay and so on—is effective. Both boys and girls benefit from developing concentration skills. Three of the big skills required for success in school—concentration, sequencing (or keeping things in the right order), and memory—can be developed with the help of parents. The easiest way of doing this is to play games with them, like cards, chess, dominoes, and battleships.

Manipulator alert!

This is the stage when Manipulators can be prone to perfectionism and bullying. This can mean they won't try things they are not sure they are good at. And they can put down others. Emphasize having a go rather than always focusing on outcomes.

Development timeline

Age	What's happening
Nine and ten	The shift from child to adolescent occurs around this time for some bright kids
	Interest patterns change quickly
	For some, an insatiable pattern of instant gratification develops
	Play occurs in friendship clusters—boys and girls are fairly separate
	Bullying can peak around this time as friendships change

Developing friendship skills

Primary schools often find that bullying increases around eight years of age as children jostle for position with peers. This continues to be a common issue until 13 years old or thereabouts. For this reason, help your child develop a range of friendships, ideally some in school and some out of school. Developing the skills of being a good friend helps children to not only fit in at this stage, but also sets them up for success in careers and relationships later on.

Many bright children don't develop friendship skills easily and may need considerable assistance in this area. Some of the key skills are:

- An awareness of the feelings of other people and how a child's own behavior impacts those feelings. Parents can help to point out how others might be feeling, and empower their child to help that person feel better. These are the building blocks of empathy and compassion. See also Chapter 21.

- An awareness of their own feelings. Bright children often emphasize action over emotion and are relatively poor at knowing how they feel. Parents can help them to identify their own feelings.

- Having a range of interests that enable them to talk to a variety of people.

- Having ways of managing their competitive nature by learning about collaboration and teamwork, and by understanding that others' successes are not a threat.

Takeaways

- Early to mid-childhood is an important time for social interaction, and having a range of friends is valuable.
- Don't allow anxieties about school to become a pattern.
- Make sure bright kids get to try out lots of different activities during this stage.

10
Late primary school

"Children aren't happy with nothing to ignore,
And that's what parents were created for."

Ogden Nash

Up to the age of nine or ten, a child's brain continues to be twice as active as an adult's. Around the age of nine, peer relationships seem to predominate. It's at this point that we start to see the brain gearing up for adolescence. Many of the neurological changes that occur in the brain during the teenage years commence well before a child gets to high school—a fact that any primary-school teacher will confirm with a sad nod of the head.

While the early onset of puberty is often viewed with dismay by adults, it may actually benefit some young people. Early maturers score slightly higher on IQ tests than their later-maturing counterparts, and this small advantage appears to persist into adulthood.

During these years, the brain starts to slow down. An eight- or nine-year-old's brain runs at about twice the speed that yours does; between eight and 18, it slows down to its adult running rate.

Following this is a stage in which the world is simplified into two basic states: "boy germs" and "girl germs." Where I grew up, all the guys would hang out on the playground, play football, or play marbles, while the girls did something strange with elastic that involved chanting.

The division of the sexes is very clear at this stage, and just when you think you've got it all sorted out—when you've got all the guys on the field or all the girls out with the elastic, and never the twain shall meet; when you've got the sign that says "No Boys [or Girls] Allowed"—then puberty comes along to change everything.

Here's a few suggestions:

- Build goodwill in families.
- Discourage and divert from aggressive acts.
- Couple high expectations with high faith in the child.
- Limit the carbohydrate intake.
- Broaden friendship groups.
- Try to get bright children into the habit of cooperating with family and mixing with a range of people.
- Stop them settling into a repetitive pattern of angry and aggressive behavior by defusing potential battlegrounds early on or dealing with confrontations quickly.

Debaters

Families can feel like international courts of appeal if they have Debater children. Try to keep things fair and routine.

Development timeline

Age	What's happening		
Eleven and twelve	Rate of physical development becomes a factor in friendships	Self-esteem years	Late-developing boys and early-developing girls are most likely to have trouble

Late childhood and early adolescence is a time of grief and loss—the child is alone in a way that she never was during childhood. Part of the loneliness of this time is due to her sense of belonging getting seriously confused. It gets confused because a new identity is breaking through the shell of childhood.

Part of this new upsurge is to do with identity formation—who she is as a person. Both boys and girls feel pressured to grow up faster than they can, and this pressure becomes focused on what they want to do with their lives—the task of realizing their dreams. This acceleration of life leaves many victims in its wake: for too many young people, life becomes a problem to be solved rather than a mystery to be unraveled. The role of parents is to protect their child's childhood, to ensure they are not exposed to the pressures, lures, and experiences of adulthood too early.

Takeaways

- The late primary years are a time when bright kids can be rushed out of childhood.
- As bright kids often want to be the first to try things, parents need to diligently monitor their children at this stage.
- The presence of parents decreases the likelihood of age-inappropriate activities.

11

Adolescence

A dolescents are a mystery to many adults—especially their parents. It is a time when three of the great changes of human life occur:

1. the ability to reproduce,
2. the establishment of an identity, and
3. the formal commencement of logical, rational, reasoned thought.

However, the attainment of logical thinking is fairly patchy from where I sit, and some people don't seem to attain it till the age of 28 or thereabouts.

There is a long history of successful people having fairly dodgy adolescent years, and this has been reflected in their school reports. For example: in the early Seventies, Stephen Fry—the English actor—received a report on which his headmaster wrote, "He has glaring faults and they have certainly glared at us this term." And Norman Wisdom, the actor, got a report that said, "The boy is every inch a fool, but luckily for him he's not very tall."

So let's take a walk through the brain and the mind of your average adolescent. Now this is dangerous territory indeed.

The likelihood of tripping over the odd torrid sexual fantasy, encountering an obsession with privacy that would baffle the most secretive hermit, or the risk of being crushed by the wild pendulum of mood swings awaits us.

Let's have a look at some of the major changes.

Synaptic pruning

It is always worth thinking about the biological and evolutionary underpinnings of development and learning. I was recently having a discussion with a group of freshman boys which went like this: "What? ... Dunno ... Alright ... S'pose ... As if ... Whatever!"

Between 10 years of age and puberty, the brain ruthlessly destroys its weakest connections, preserving only those that experience has shown to be useful. The adage here is "use it or lose it"—and this applies at any age. "Synaptic pruning" continues throughout life, but occurs mostly during the late childhood and teenage years so that the synapses that carry the most messages get stronger and the weaker ones get cut out. As many as 30,000 synapses may be lost per second over the entire cortex in the early adolescent brain, leading to an ultimate loss of almost one half of the synapses that were present in the pre-adolescent period. All this helps with refinement and specialization. This is why the experiences we give children and young people between their ninth and eighteenth years are so important.

Development timeline		
Age	**What's happening**	
Thirteen	Exclusive friendship groups among girls	Self-absorption Privacy from parents while being reliant on them
Fourteen	Sexual identity Popularity Differentiation	

Jerome Bruner has suggested that the reason humans are dependent for so long is so they can learn about their specific social environment. We survive by learning how to get on in almost any setting, by living by our wits, and by being extraordinarily adaptable.

Development timeline		
Age	**What's happening**	
Fifteen	Emotions are at the basis of most decision making	Risky behaviors to gain peer acceptance

The brain at this time is re-structuring in order to become cleverer and more efficient. It is important to capitalize on this by helping young people to create patterns of thinking and habits of learning that are productive. By doing this, we put into place trajectories of thinking and learning that lead to success.

THE PASSIVE RESISTER

Restructuring and the frontal lobe

The second thing that happens in an adolescent's brain is that the frontal lobe—the bit that helps us to plan, consider, control impulses, make wise judgments; in short, to be kind, caring, considerate people—is the last bit to mature. In fact someone probably should hang a sign on the frontal lobe of most early adolescents saying "Closed for construction." The frontal lobe is being restructured at this time in a way that prepares a child for adult life.

If you are wondering what the big deal with the frontal lobe is, it's really the frontal lobe that allows us to be civilized and human. Susan Greenfield estimates that over the course of history the size of the frontal lobe in humans has increased by 29 percent, compared with 17 percent in chimpanzees and 3 percent in cats.

This not only tells you a lot about why a hungry cat won't leave well enough alone, it should also give you pause to think compassionately about your ancestors, who had to spend their lives hanging around with a group of eternally impulsive and erratic teenagers of various ages while working out a way to produce evolution's latest upgrade—you! I hope you are dutifully grateful.

Development timeline	
Age	**What's happening**
Sixteen	Accepting their physique and a masculine or feminine role
	Developing more supportive relationships with their peers
	Gaining independence from their parents and teachers
	Often the organizational demands of school challenge them
	Bright kids often have a "Jekyll and Hyde" lifestyle happening at this time: publicly they are delightful, at home they can be monsters

So the early adolescent's frontal lobe has essentially gone missing in action for a time. This means that teenagers' brains are all tuned up for emotions, fighting, running away, and romance, but not so well tuned up for planning, controlling impulses, and forward thinking. Some parents forget this. They wouldn't dream of giving their teenager free access to their life savings, but they will quite frequently leave them in charge of a $300,000 house full of fine furniture and still be stunned by the results!

Parents need to *be* their teenage children's frontal lobe. Asking an adolescent to do a lot of forward planning is like asking a toddler to study physics. This is also the reason why too much freedom too soon does not seem to help too many young people.

Early teenagers are yet to grow into themselves. The average teenager gains 45 pounds and grows almost a foot and a half in the space of four or five years. I'm sure many of you know the sensation of being in a room with a group of young people who seem to be a clumsy jumble of elbows, knees, pimples, and groins. Just as they haven't grown into their bodies, they haven't quite grown into their brains, either.

It's almost as if teenagers at this stage are like a very powerful, juiced-up sports car: great acceleration, terrific lines, great sex appeal, but very poor brakes ... oh, and a driver with the road sense of an earwig.

Development timeline	
Age	**What's happening**
Seventeen	Seeking economic independence
	Selecting an occupation
	Developing intellectual skills and concepts necessary for civic competence
	Desiring and achieving socially responsible behavior

Implications for parents of bright adolescents

- Adolescents are *not* mini–adults.
- Don't expect them to show a lot of forethought or planning.
- The brain is restructuring to become more efficient, and we need to capitalize on this. Help them to develop habits and routines that allow them to work smarter, not harder.

Emotions

A couple of other interesting things are happening for adolescents. The first is that hormones become more powerful, and adolescents' brains show more activity in the emotional parts of the brain (known as the limbic system) than they do in the planning and the impulse-control parts (known as the frontal lobe and the pre-frontal cortex, respectively). This means that adolescents learn best when there is emotion involved! Adolescents remember stuff about themselves and stuff that is relevant to their life situations. As Homer Simpson would say, "D'oh!"

One father I spoke to wanted to put a sign on his daughter's bedroom door that stated, "Warning—Wide Mood Swings!" Adolescents *like* intensity, excitement, and arousal. They are drawn to music, passion, horror films.

Around this time adolescents usually give off exaggerated secondary signals such as sneers, rolling eyes, and sighing. Unwise parents and teachers respond to these.

This is why it is *absolutely pointless* arguing with teenagers.

Development timeline	
Age	**What's happening**
Eighteen	Building conscious values in harmony with the world Building the skills for college—stress management, energy management, time management, and organizational skills

Not only are they emotionally charged, they are also lousy at reading other people's emotions, particularly fear.

It may well be that the brain develops best when allowed to play, linger, and persist in areas of interest, and that this may especially be so when the early adolescent is in the company of someone whose opinion he cares about.

Implications for parents of bright adolescents

Two fairly useless questions to ask early teenagers are:

1. "What were you thinking?" (because they probably weren't)

2. "Couldn't you see she [or he] was frightened?" (because they can't).

Teenagers do well with high levels of supervision: they need you as much as, if not a bit more than, when they were little.

Myelination

Another thing that is happening in adolescents' brains is myelination. Myelin is a fatty material that wraps itself around the axons of brain cells and helps the brain to communicate quickly and efficiently. Simply put, it turbo-charges thinking. (In multiple sclerosis, it is the myelin sheath that breaks down, causing such devastating effects for sufferers.)

It is during the adolescent years that myelin is put into place—it increases by about 100 percent during this time. Two areas of the brain that are extensively undergoing myelination are the hippocampus, which has to do with memory, and the cingulate, which involves emotions. This research explains two of the great mysteries of life with teenagers. For years I would watch parents say to their adolescent children, "What are you thinking about?," only to receive a blank look, a shrug of the shoulders, and a "Dunno." I always thought they were putting it on; now I really think they don't know. They weren't thinking at all. That blank look was completely justified: they were only reacting.

The research indicating the level of myelination in the cingulate also points to solving the mystery of some family interactions. The cingulate is involved in moral reasoning. The relative inability of early adolescents to think through consequences and measure their responses again partly explains why, in family therapy, parents lament how their teenager goes "absolutely berserk," "over the top," "ballistic," and so on when asked to do something minor like take out the trash. Teenagers have little sense of perspective.

Increased affiliation with peers

It's not going to come as news to most of you that the adolescent brain is not only tumultuously emotional, it is also incredibly social. As neuroscientist Linda Spear points out, most species show an alteration in social behavior around the time of adolescence. Play fighting and play behavior increase before declining as sexual maturity is reached.

During an average week, adolescents have been reported to spend close to one third of their time awake talking with peers, but only 8 percent talking with adults.

Teenagers are nothing if not great imitators. Fashion, music, lip gloss, heavy deodorant—it's all around you! As well as being great imitators, they are wary in case they lose peer approval. Many have two worlds: the world of peers, where they need to be cool, compact, and calculating; and the world of family, where they can still be young and make mistakes. Parents shouldn't expect teenagers to behave with their peers in the same way they behave with them.

> ## Competitors watch out!
>
> Churchillian kids can take loss and failure very badly in the senior years of school. The risk is that they can give up challenging the world and disappear in a haze, literally. The realm of drugs is not a good one for these kids. Look for opportunities for them to have adventures, preferably involving physical challenges and new peer groups.

Sensitivity to stress

The decision-making ability of adolescents may be more vulnerable to disruptions by the stresses and strains of everyday living than that of adults. Adolescents are often sleep-deprived, which may in turn increase their vulnerability to stress. Teenagers may have more negative life experiences (friendship changes, alterations in romantic liaisons, schoolwork) than adults, which they tend to view more negatively and have less control over. This may well increase their sense of helplessness.

The more negative life events an adolescent has, the more likely he is to engage in problem behaviors and the less likely he is to engage in a wide range of positive activities.

Adolescents display considerably poorer cognitive performance under time-limited situations than under optimal test conditions. This means that they can perform poorly on exams. If this occurs, make sure they don't use their own exam performance as a measure of their ability.

Development timeline	
Age	**What's happening**
Early adulthood	Frustration as the desire for autonomy and independence is thwarted by the need for further education or financial support from family
	Family conflict can rise in the "terrible twenties" as different views about sex, romance, and household contributions abound
	Keep them busy and actively involved in life

Increased risk taking

Adolescents are risk takers. They love reckless behavior, sensation seeking, and risk taking. In one study, 80 percent of 11-and-a-half- to 15-year-olds exhibited one or more problem behaviors in a month, such as disobeying parents, school misconduct, substance use, and antisocial acts, including theft or fighting.

Risk taking during adolescence is normal. Risk takers feel more accepted by peers and view risk taking as fun. Non-risk takers are seen as anxious and overcontrolled.

Adolescents take risks for a variety of reasons:

- sensations of novelty—the desire for an adrenaline rush may be particularly strong,
- change or intensity of experience,
- to improve chances for sex,
- to reduce unhappiness, help them cope with stress, and
- risk taking can be seen as an attempt to gain real-life experiences of yourself and your environment.

Dare Devils

There is no way you'll stop them taking risks. You've just got to find fun, positive ways for them to do so. Involve them in whitewater rafting, mountaineering, motocross, surfing, martial arts—anything you can think of!

THAT'S WHERE I LEFT MY BALL!

"People don't learn to try to succeed in socially undesirable ways until they have learned that they cannot succeed in socially desirable ways."

Alfred Adler

This is a very important point for bright kids. *Find acceptable ways for them to take risks and to achieve success.*

Risk taking and drug experimentation

One way of relieving boredom is substance abuse. Some exploratory drug use is usual during adolescence. Worryingly, teenagers may become dependent more rapidly than adults. After peer substance use, perceived levels of stress most strongly predict adolescent alcohol and drug use.

Alcohol and cigarettes are often considered gateway drugs that can lead to more illicit drug abuse. Early use of alcohol powerfully predicts later alcohol abuse and dependence; it may also alter brain development.

Other risk factors—i.e., violence, criminal activity, risky sexual behaviors, teen pregnancy, and dangerous driving—cluster around early initiation into alcohol use, so it is worth trying to delay your child's experimentation with alcohol and drugs.

Anger and aggression

Aggressive behavior peaks during adolescence in a number of primate species. Aggression has its origins in the limbic areas, and particularly the amygdala, which relates to the emotions and shapes the "fight or flight" response (i.e., it works to defend you against threats or it tells you to run away from them). When emotional, adolescents have lower activity in their frontal lobes and more activity in the amygdala than adults. This means they are all set up for arguing and not so well set up for thinking things through.

The life trajectories of bright kids

Another way of viewing how bright kids develop is to look at the common pathways that kids follow as they grow up.

Pathway 1: Sailing through. It is important to remember that most bright kids get through their childhood and adolescent years well. Sure, there is going to be the odd rough spot. As with all teenagers, they will worry about getting a date, having too many pimples and not enough freedom. But most young people like their family, get on well with their parents most of the time, and maintain a positive sense of self.

Pathway 2: Puberty troubles. Around the onset of puberty is a time of lowered functioning for many bright kids as hormones, body growth, increased irritability, and mood swings can dominate their relationships during this time.

Pathways of growth

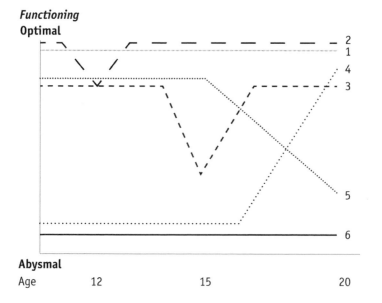

Functioning

Optimal

2
1
4
3

5

6

Abysmal

Age   12   15   20

Pathway 3: Mid-adolescent conniptions. This trajectory is notorious in schools as a Year 8 or 9 phenomenon. This is a subgroup of bright kids who engage in aggressive or delinquent behaviors in their middle adolescent years. The great fear often expressed is that these young people will go on to take up lives of criminal behavior or drug addiction. Experimentation with risk taking is common with this group, and may be a way of expressing autonomy. Generally, these bright kids do not adopt a broader negative lifestyle.

Pathway 4: Turnaround. Life events and opportunities can contribute to an upturn in functioning. Some bright kids, as they grow, develop, and gain autonomy, are able to link up with a more adaptable adult. Others speak of a particular teacher or counselor who was able to inspire and support them; someone who believed in them.

Pathway 5: Adolescent decline. This is a group of young people who, as they reach their mid-adolescence, begin a decline often involving depression, aggression, and substance abuse that deteriorates through the late-adolescent years. These young people congregate with a troubled group of young people as their only way of experiencing social regard and success. Their belief in their inability to fit in and to have some sense of personal success leads them to behave in ways that invoke in others responses that confirm this position of despair.

Pathway 6: Consistently poor functioning. This pathway relates to those who enter adolescence with a history throughout their childhood of problems or disorder. These young people have often grown up in poorly functioning families in the presence of substance abuse or violence.

What does all this mean for parents of bright adolescents?

A number of things:

- Realize that children and adolescents are not just a smaller version of adults. The growing brain is in transition: it differs neurochemically and anatomically from adults'.

- Realize that these changes can continue into the mid- to late twenties.

- Remember that teenagers' frontal lobes are "closed for construction." Don't expect teenagers to show a lot of forethought, planning, or consideration for others.

- Grab them by their emotions. If you want children and adolescents to learn, make it emotionally relevant to them. Use their favorite TV shows to spark their interest.

- Bombard them with positives. This is the age where motivation gets tricky. Use rewards. Damn it, use anything you can think of to keep them intrigued. If, at the end of these years, they can say, "I like life, it's fun, and I can succeed (and my parents aren't that bad)," you deserve a medal.

- Tell them that you love them, and keep telling them.
- Be aware that too much freedom is not good.
- Last but not least, never underestimate your power. Bright kids need someone around them—an adult who has more options than they do, someone they may battle with, but someone who ultimately they imitate and emulate. And, believe it or not, that someone is you. The best way of maintaining at least the illusion of having more options than they have is to know how to repair the family when you need to.

Takeaways

- The early teen years can be a clash point for families with bright kids.
- It's important not to confuse your bright kid's demands for more independence with him or her needing you less.
- Bright kids at this age need lots and lots of time with their parents.

Part Three

How to create change

From time to time, all families slip into patterns that are less than helpful. With bright kids in the family, this becomes almost inevitable. The following chapters represent the distillation of over 25 years of clinical practice working with bright kids and their families. They also contain ideas, suggestions, and approaches from hundreds of thousands of parents who have attended workshops to discuss their delights, dilemmas, and disasters in raising bright kids.

As clear as I hope you find the ideas in the next few chapters to be, every family is different. This means you'll need to adapt these ideas to your family. No one will ever know your children as well as you do. This means that you are in the best position to judge whether any of the specific strategies I outline are appropriate to your situation.

So grab a cup of something warm to drink, a snack of something nice, and be prepared to read with a view to working out what *you* can use. One little bit of advice, though, before we begin:

Be bold.

12

The chemistry behind their moods

Bright children get into moods. When you are parenting bright kids, reading moods and knowing how to change them becomes really important.

You know about moods. You've been in one yourself. For example, you might be having a day when you are not your usual bubbly self and someone says something to you that would normally cheer you up but instead you reply, "Whatever ...." Or maybe you are in a great mood, charging through life and feeling good and someone says something to you that would normally upset you but instead you reply, "Doesn't matter," "It's okay," or "It will be fine."

If you have a bright kid, you know *all* about moods. Have you ever had the experience of watching a child come home from school with a dark cloud over his head, and thought to yourself, "It's going to be a long, long afternoon and it's not going to get any better"? (Or words to that effect.) Ever had your child wake up in a foul mood, and thought to yourself, "He got up on the wrong side of the bed and it's not going to get any better"? (Or words to that effect.)

We are all in the business of mood changing. Parents of bright kids need to become experts in the business of creating and changing moods.

The really important thing to know is:

Until you change their mood, you can't change their behavior.

When you are in a mood, you don't have many behaviors to choose from. A kid who is tired and grumpy can either be irritable and annoying or sullen and switched off. Happiness and compliance are not options that are available to them at that moment. If you expect a bright kid to shift from angry to happy without something major happening in between, you are living in fantasy land.

Let's repeat that key idea: until you change their mood, you can't change their behavior.

The moods that we all experience aren't just to do with whatever is happening that day. They also have a lot to do with the chemicals running around in our brains and bodies.

The invisible world of body and brain chemistry has as much power to shift emotions as does a happy or sad event. When parents hear this they often heave a sigh of relief: it explains why some behaviors come "out of the blue" without any warning or causative event.

While parents of bright kids don't need to become experts in neurochemistry and physiology, there are a few key brain chemicals that are well worth knowing about. This knowledge has the power to change your family.

Two brain chemicals parents of bright kids would usually like to see *less* of are adrenaline and cortisol.

Two brain chemicals parents of bright kids would usually like to see *more* of are dopamine and serotonin.

Adrenaline = action (all pumped up with nowhere to go)

Adrenaline is at least partly responsible for the revved-up high. Living on adrenaline energy causes people to burn the candle at both ends. It makes people less flexible and it makes it harder for bright kids to change their moods.

When there is a lot of adrenaline, the amygdala—the fight/ flight area of the brain—is very active. In fact this part of the brain can get so active that it takes over almost everything else. It is very powerful. You might know this yourself. Perhaps you've had a day where someone in the morning said something to you that was mean or nasty and you just weren't your usual self for the rest of the day. That is at least partly because you were threatened and your adrenaline levels were raised and your fight/flight mechanism kicked in.

Once a bright kid gets an adrenaline rush, trying to change her behavior is a complete waste of time—until you've lessened the amount of adrenaline. There are clear signs that a bright kid is having an adrenaline rush (see the box below).

Having a family life where a lot of repetition and rituals occur can lessen adrenaline. Giving an adrenaline-affected bright kid a clear, calm message that "this is the way we do things in this home" helps her to feel safe. Less stimulation, such as quiet times, can also help.

Every so often you might want to increase the amount of adrenaline because it is an energizer. One way to do this is time trials. For example, "Let's see if we can clean up this room in ten minutes, and then we'll play a game."

Likely signs of high levels of adrenaline

- Exhibits silly, "hyper" behavior
- Has difficulty getting to sleep
- Has lots of energy
- Runs off if upset
- Has squabbles and little conflicts
- Has difficulty in shifting attention
- Is reluctant to try new things
- Shows lots of busyness but not much gets done.

Cortisol cowboys and cowgirls

Cortisol is the other main neurochemical and hormone worth watching out for. Cortisol is the stress hormone, and it gets released with adrenaline. Terrific, huh? Stressed *and* revved up.

Cortisol lowers language functioning. Have you ever been shocked speechless where you temporarily couldn't put your thoughts into words? What happened was that cortisol flooded into the Broca's area of your brain—the language production center—shutting it down for a time. Bright kids who are under lots of stress often have great difficulty putting their thoughts into words. That's why you sometimes get monosyllabic grunts, especially from teenagers.

Cortisol lessens people's ability to shift gears. It makes them snappy and easily rattled. It also reduces the ability to filter irrelevant information, which partly explains why people who are stressed can find it difficult to prioritize. There are clear signs that bright kids are cortisol cowboys or cowgirls (see the box below).

Parents of bright kids will often want to lessen the amount of cortisol and, instead, to have a calm and happy life. Alongside family routines and rituals, making children feel safe from violence, ridicule, or humiliation lessens cortisol. Ensuring that bright kids do not have too much sugar and do drink enough water also helps to reduce cortisol. Getting enough sleep lowers both adrenaline and cortisol.

Fluorescent lighting has been associated with elevated levels of cortisol. Families with bright kids would be better off with indirect lighting such as lamps.

Likely signs of high levels of cortisol

- Has difficulty expressing thoughts
- Is worried and watchful
- Is easily upset
- Is on edge

- Is defensive
- Overreacts to things
- May be a bit more smelly than usual (stress makes perspiration more sour)
- Finds it difficult to prioritize.

Dopamine

Dopamine creates the switched-on, pumped-up state. Dopamine is good for pleasure and motivation: it's the party animal of the neurochemical world.

Dopamine helps people change moods. It approaches adult levels somewhere between six and nine years, then lowers during the teenage years. This explains why teenagers can be harder to motivate than younger children. There are clear signs that bright kids are down on dopamine (see the box on page 90).

Dopamine also plays an important role in shifting and directing attention and concentration. There is evidence that some families may have patterns where they have difficulties with this. In these families, there is a need to increase dopamine levels.

Parents of bright kids may want to increase dopamine. To do so, try some of these ideas:

- sports that involve repetitive movements such as table tennis, swimming, handball, and marching
- solving challenges and problems—asking your children to help you out by working out a solution to some family issue
- social interaction—even the fairly reclusive Passive Resisters will benefit from an increase in dopamine when they get to mix socially
- rewards—inducements, bribery, call it what you will, it works!
- dietary supplements of tyrosine and Omega 3 and 6, which have also been associated with increases in dopamine.

Likely signs of low levels of dopamine

- Has difficulty getting focused
- Is unmotivated
- Is not proud of accomplishments
- Is lethargic and tired
- Is uninterested and won't try things out
- Finds it unsettling or difficult to shift from one activity to another

Serotonin

Serotonin is the most powerful antidepressant known to humankind, and whether you are a bright kid or her parent, you could do with more of this. While dopamine gives you the pumped-up high, serotonin is the quiet achiever. It is the slow high, and it accompanies calm, considered decision making.

There are clear signs that bright kids may be low on serotonin (see the box on the next page). Low levels of serotonin are also linked to depression.

Serotonin can be increased by exercise. Whereas activities with repetitive movements particularly increase dopamine, exercise of almost any kind will raise levels of serotonin. Giving positive, warm feedback also increases serotonin, as does giving bright kids some choice, control, and areas of responsibility.

Some bright kids lead very pressured lives where they are required to fit in to someone else's schedule. Have times of the week at home when the pressure is off. When you do as you please at the rate you please, serotonin levels rise. Sleep is a big serotonin builder.

Too much caffeine and artificial sweeteners such as aspartame are toxic to serotonin. Try to keep bright kids away from these.

If there seems to be a strong pattern of low serotonin, a psychological assessment may be beneficial.

Likely signs of low levels of serotonin

- Is sullen and uncommunicative
- Is hard to get going in the morning
- Is hard to please
- Doesn't respond to praise
- Everything seems to be a bother
- Is sad or depressed
- Needs a reason to do things (asks "Why do we have to ...?")
- Avoids eye contact
- Wants to disappear from family activities.

Parenting strategies likely to increase dopamine	Parenting strategies likely to decrease adrenaline
• Do enjoyable activities. • Play challenging games. • Focus on what you like and love about your child more than what you don't like. • Use humor. • Plan some positive family goals that everyone can look forward to. • Move your child to a new setting or change what she is doing. • Learn a new skill together.	• Devote some time of each week to organization. • Allow "lazy time," i.e., time each week when there is nothing planned and no pressure to do anything. • If you are arguing, stop it. Solve it later if you can.

Parenting strategies likely to increase serotonin	Parenting strategies likely to decrease cortisol
<ul><li>Praise your child.</li><li>Be affectionate.</li><li>Create positive time.</li><li>Play games and exercises.</li><li>Avoid foods and drinks with artificial sweeteners.</li><li>Celebrate life and your family.</li><li>Make a big thing of positive moments.</li><li>Eat breakfast (more protein and less carbohydrate if possible).</li></ul>	<ul><li>Do more listening and less talking (yes, you!).</li><li>Play relaxing music.</li><li>Speak calmly.</li><li>Eliminate caffeine from their diet (and lessen it in your own).</li><li>Drink more water.</li><li>Get enough sleep.</li></ul>

Takeaways

- Neurochemistry plays a powerful role in creating behavior.
- Adrenaline, cortisol, dopamine, and serotonin are four key neurochemicals that influence what bright kids do.
- Learning to read the neurochemical signs places parents in a powerful position to change behavior.

13

Eight important mood changers

Now that we've got a nodding acquaintance with dopamine, serotonin, adrenaline, and cortisol, let's have a look at how we can use them to help bright kids improve their mood.

Mood changer #1: Sleep

Bright kids need plenty of sleep. It means you get some time off, it means they learn better at school, and it means they are easier to live with! Need more convincing? The amount of sleep that is ideal is nine and a quarter hours per night.

Surveys of bright kids indicate they do not get enough sleep. Access to mobile phones, computers, and televisions in bedrooms are all enemies of sleep. Keep electronics out of bedrooms.

Many bright kids are overstimulated in the evenings and find it difficult to settle. The production of the sleep chemical, melatonin, is stopped if you are exposed to bright lights. In order to help children to sleep well, lower the lighting of an evening in your home or use indirect lighting such as lamps.

The quality of sleep of many bright kids is also a concern. Some seem to want to pile on the blankets to the point of almost cooking themselves. Once they have fallen asleep, check that they are not too hot or too cool.

Sleep is also important for learning. Memory consolidation occurs while we are asleep and is thought to be associated with dream or REM ("rapid eye movement") sleep. During the normal eight or nine hours of sleep, five REM cycles occur. If a bright kid is getting only five or six hours of sleep, she loses the last two REM cycles, and thereby reduces the amount of time the brain has to consolidate information into long-term storage.

The amount of sleep we get directly relates to how much serotonin we have and how vulnerable to stress we are. If getting enough sleep is a problem, then having a daytime nap is useful. Having a nap can be just as effective in promoting learning and memory as a full night's sleep. This is certainly the case if you can have a 90-minute nap, but even 60 minutes will do if you dream in that time. The effect of a nap is similar to going to bed early, which has also been shown to enhance learning.

Some tips for making sure they get a good night's sleep

- No caffeine after 4 p.m. (that includes soft drinks and energy drinks with lots of caffeine).

- No vigorous exercise in the two hours before sleep time.

- If they report feeling tired in the evening, it is a good idea to ask them to go to bed. If they push through that tiredness, they won't have another sleep wave for another 90 minutes.

- Keep televisions, mobile phones, and computers out of bedrooms.

- Remember, there is no such thing as a sleep bank. Just because they slept 10 hours last night doesn't mean they can cope with only six tonight.

- Make sure they don't get overheated in bed.

- Don't get too stressed if they are unable to sleep. Just having them lie quietly in a darkened room is rejuvenating.

Know your downtime

The time when you learn least well and the time you could use a power nap are roughly the same. To work out your downtime, take the mid-point of your sleeping pattern, go forward 12 hours, and that's the time. So if you sleep from 10 p.m. to 7 a.m., the mid-point of your sleep is 2:30 a.m., which means that around 2:30 p.m. is your most likely downtime. In fact, surveys in schools indicate that 2:30 p.m. is the most common downtime for late childhood and adolescence.

Knowing your child's likely downtime is pretty handy. There is little point saying to a child who is having her downtime, "Have you got any homework?" It's also useful to know your own downtime. If you are having your downtime and they are having theirs, and you decide to have a discussion about a difficult issue, you are wasting your time. It would be better to go for a walk or do something different. Downtime lasts about half an hour either side of the time you've worked out.

It's also important for parents of bright kids to get enough sleep. Bright kids often live life in the fast lane, awaken revved up and ready to go, and don't slow down till late in the evening. It's easy to become sleep-deprived when parenting at the best of times. Sleep deprivation makes us all more vulnerable to stress, more easily rattled, and crankier. Work out a strategy to get the amount of sleep you need.

Mood changer #2: Lighting

As mentioned, fluorescent lighting can make bright kids more agitated. Natural or indirect lighting such as lamps is best. Try not to have bright kids studying under florescent lighting. Children in classrooms lit with full-spectrum rather than fluorescent lights have fewer missed school days. Fluorescent light raises cortisol levels in the bloodstream and can suppress the immune system.

Getting outside more is also important for mood. Most of the winter blues as well as many winter illnesses can be explained by not being outside enough. Open-air activity also helps bright kids to burn up some excess energy.

A common measure of light intensity is the "lux." Natural sunlight ranges from 2,000 lux on a cloudy day to 100,000 lux on a sunny day. If you are mostly indoors, you will only get about 100 lux. Some bright kids get irritable and sad when they are not exposed to enough sunlight. A 150- to 200-watt globe equals 2,500 lux, and there is evidence that using a bright light in the day improves mood. Of course, even better than using a light is to get outdoors.

Lowering the level of lighting in your home a few hours before sleep time makes it easier for everyone to get a sound night's sleep, which makes them less vulnerable to stress and less irritable.

Mood changer #3: Diet

Food is a very powerful drug. You know that! That's why we like to go to fancy restaurants and eat fine foods and drink fine wines.

One of the fastest ways to change anyone's mood is to feed and water them. Just having a glass of water lowers the amount of cortisol. If there is nothing else that you can do with a stressed, bright kid, offer her a drink of water. If she won't have one, have one yourself. You'll need it.

Julia Ross, in her fascinating book *The Mood Cure*, writes about the importance of increasing proteins and lessening carbohydrates at breakfast time. Having this type of breakfast increases concentration and memory. A diet that is rich in an amino acid called tryptophan also works to prevent depression; tryptophan is found in many foods, such as turkey, lean beef, and almonds. These foods give you a higher tryptophan level in your bloodstream. Tryptophan synthesizes in the body into serotonin. You can give most bright kids a natural antidepressant effect by putting them on this type of diet.

This will be particularly effective if you can at the same time lessen the amounts of caffeine and artificially sweetened foods and drinks they have.

Mood changer #4: Movement

The more I work with bright kids, the more I become convinced that the body has memories. It seems that particular postures, stances or positions bring with them specific memories. A bright kid with a slumped posture might access memories of tiredness or sadness more easily, while one with a grimacing face might recall anger or fear.

Part of changing the mood is to move your child—not by pushing and shoving, but by saying something like, "I can see you are upset. I've got to go to the kitchen—walk with me and tell me what's happening." By moving him, you are shifting the pattern.

Many bright kids are fairly active and not so interested in deep discussions about feelings. Walking side by side with them and hearing about how things are for them won't resolve whatever the problem is, but it will make it more solvable.

Mood changer #5: Music

Millions of teenagers are not wrong. Music changes your mood and your brain functioning.

Music is a whole-brain activity—it has a powerful influence over emotion, learning, and analysis. Some studies have related Mozart's music to increased intelligence levels: students who listened to Mozart's Sonata for Two Pianos in D major for 10 minutes raised their test scores in abstract and spatial reasoning. Pachabel's Canon, and baroque music in general, have also been identified as being associated with relaxation and enhanced performance.

Listening to music may also alter brain organization: four-years-olds who listened to one hour of classical music each day had EEG (electroencephalogram) results that suggested more brain coherence. They also spent more time in an alpha state—that is, calm, relaxed, and alert.

Learning to play a musical instrument is also beneficial. For example, playing the piano increases spatial awareness and the ability to think ahead. Learning music also increases listening and memory skills.

Try to match kids to instruments they are likely to succeed at. For example, the clarinet, piano, and advanced guitar require fine motor skills, whereas the trumpet, drums, and percussion require gross motor skills. Playing a musical instrument can be a terrific way of expressing the emotions that bright kids sometimes find difficult to put into words. The repetitive movements involved in playing some instruments may also raise dopamine levels.

Having music playing around the house when bright kids are breakfasting or when they come home from school indicates to them that they are in a different place (i.e., not at school) and can help them to change mood.

Mood changer #6: Television and videos

Television changes mood. Anyone who has ever flopped down in front of a television set and zonked out knows this.

Children in the later primary and early secondary years often have phenomenal amounts of screen time. Twenty-two percent watch television for more than three hours a day, and 14 percent also spend more than three hours playing computer games.

Television models impulsive acting-out behaviors to children. Those of us old enough to remember *The Dobie Gillis Show* will recall that Dobie was often depicted in the still pose of Rodin's The Thinker. Incorporating a similarly inactive character in a television show today would be unthinkable.

However, a study of over 1,000,000 students in Israel found the relationship between TV viewing and educational attainment to be complex. A small amount of TV (up to 1.4 hours per day, or 10 hours per week) is positively associated with academic achievement; beyond that, it is negative, especially for students aged between 10 and 17 years.

The ideal amount of television differs according to how old your child is. There is increasing research showing that television viewing of any extended duration impairs the concentration of children under two. A nine-year-old can watch up to two hours a day, a 13-year-old one-and-a-half hours, and for 17-year-olds, the ideal amount of television viewing drops to just half an hour each day.

Mood changer #7: Computer games

Anyone who has ever watched an irritable, unfocused, unmotivated bright kid switch on a computer game and become focused, alert, and goal-oriented knows that these games have an incredible power to change moods.

I describe today's kids as the "Click and Go" generation— the Baby Boomlets who were born with a mouse in their hand and who have grown up with the expectation of immediate gratification, instant outcome, and continual entertainment. One of the factors influencing their lives has been video and computer games. There are both positive and negative effects of these games. On the positive side, they build hand–eye coordination and develop problem-solving skills. They can also be a form of social connection.

Boys particularly use video games in a social way by organizing LANs (local area networks) or simply by watching and discussing strategies. In many cases, boys read books full of "cheats" that guide them in how to succeed at the game. The use of video and computer games is not completely passive.

These games also give a sense of great mastery, challenge, and involvement. Children can become adventurous heroes winning battles, building cities, and conquering challenges all in the safety of their homes.

Video games are popular, and link into three of the most desired states of childhood:

1. the ability to have adult-like adventures with minimal adult involvement,

2. the ability to test yourself, and

3. the sense of being in a club of other young people who collect these games.

But the excessive playing of these games can be negative. They can be so compelling, they become addictive. I have seen some kids in therapy for whom the withdrawal of the computer resulted in a grief reaction comparable to the loss of a family member!

Also, the skills learned on these games do not appear to readily transfer into other arenas of life. Computer games are so successful at setting challenges and providing rewards that they seem to interfere with young people's ability to do this themselves. Very few of the games require creative problem solving or provide an opportunity to be an active participant in determining a story line.

The illusion can be quite strong. A 10-year-old boy I saw in counseling, when asked what sport he played, answered "Quidditch!" When I asked him how he played this sport, he looked at me pityingly and said, "On the computer, of course."

Children with low self-esteem or psychological vulnerabilities may seek solace in computer games. If you are neglected, anxious, or depressed, a place where you can build cities, win wars, and score points to become the world champion is pretty compelling. If you are experiencing powerlessness, and get even a hint of power through violent video games, you are likely to overvalue the usefulness of violence as a way of solving problems. If you continue to watch and play violent games with very few other social interactions that give you a sense of mastery, you are facing a toxic mix that leads many children to some level of violent actions.

Parents need to parent their children, and that requires them to involve their children in a variety of activities, of which the computer may be one, but certainly not the main one.

There is no research yet on the ideal amount of computer game usage. Bright kids are often drawn to computer games, which can provide a level of visual excitement.

One of the toughest transitions for a bright kid is from the computer (including computer games) to almost any other activity. For this reason, parents often say they find it best to limit the amount of computer game time to just before a meal. Food and hunger are probably the best inducements to stop a computer game. *Never* allow a bright kid to eat his meal while playing a computer game. If you do, you may never get him back to the table again.

Mood changer #8: You!

Author Jeff Conley has a wonderful expression: "taking a check-up from the neck up." That is exactly what we all need to do from time to time.

Parenting bright kids can wear the perkiest parent down. With everyone willing to chip in with their own homespun piece of advice, it can be easy to at times feel like everyone's favorite whipping post.

The first thing to do is: *get rid of your guilt!*

Guilt is woven into modern parenting. No parent can be there enough, clever enough, loving enough, giving enough, tough enough, soft enough. I remember asking one mother who was feeling guilty to list the qualities she believed a perfect mother should have. Listing an impressive array of characteristics, I asked her what the effect would be if she had taken on being a perfect mother. She laughed and responded, "The family would be financially ruined and I'd be a neurotic mess. You're right, it is impossible."

The second thing to do is: *set the tone for your home.*

Use the knowledge in this chapter to change the mood of your family. Lead by example: sleep well, eat well, live well. Not only do you deserve it; your bright kid won't take seriously your intention to tune up your family life until *you* do so.

Takeaways

- Bright kids' moods and behaviors aren't determined by their thoughts alone.
- Many other factors can help to settle them, including adequate sleep, diet, physical activity, music, limited computer usage, and *you*.

14

Stop what you are doing—Step 1

Sometimes, when family interactions get stuck, everyone falls into despair, anger, and blame, which of course only serves to make everything even more stuck.

There are times in all our families' lives when we need to re-invent and renew. This is especially true of families with bright kids because they can wear family processes out and leave in their wake feelings of resentment and smouldering weariness.

Some of you will remember The Professor from the popular television show, *Gilligan's Island*. A brilliant man, able to invent coconut compasses, a wind-powered electricity generator, not to mention a thousand other quirky creations. But somehow he never found time to either work out a way to patch the hole in the ship or build a new ship entirely.

Sometimes, in parenting bright kids, we can be like The Professor: we fix the minor everyday issues without fixing the whole thing. So rather than look at which part of the family to patch up next, I want to outline a process that has the potential to re-shape the way you relate with your bright kid.

In over 25 years of clinical practice with bright kids and their families, I have often wondered why most interventions take about six weeks before they really work. I think it takes six weeks to form a new habit.

The five-step process

The following five-step process has been trialed on thousands of families, with parents and children both routinely reporting improved outcomes. And, as I said, it generally takes around six weeks to complete.

Step 1: Stop what you are doing
Step 2: Build belonging
Step 3: Create a culture of cooperation
Step 4: Start a new dance
Step 5: The new dance

One way of thinking about it is as a family tune-up kit. When relationships have become tense and frayed, it is worth taking time to try out a different way of getting on.

During these six weeks there will be ups and downs, successful moments, and moments when you will want to tear your hair out. In fact, I can promise you there will be more downs than ups to begin with. Bright kids are often used to getting their own way, and they are not the type of people to give up an advantage easily.

At the same time, bright kids are not "bad" kids. They are simply people who have found one way of relating to the world that works for them and they've kept using that strategy. The aim of this five-step process is to give them an opportunity to flourish and widen their definition of who they are while giving you a chance to regain your calm, sane disposition.

Changing the dance

Bright children are incredibly patterned creatures! They do the same thing, in the damn same way, over and over again.

The intensity of their anger or the depth of their hostility or the degree of their frustration might be alarming, but the actual dance steps are predictable. They have fairly limited routines.

This is useful knowledge because:

> *If you change one of the dance steps,*
> *you change the entire dance.*

At first, the behavior of bright kids looks very erratic and unpredictable. Parents often make comments like, "He just loses his cool, there is no way of predicting it" or, "There is no warning, she just makes a run for it." If, however, you can sit back and watch closely, a pattern of behaviors will appear, and once you've got that bit of knowledge you can select how to shift their behaviors to help them build better life habits.

> GROUNDED FOR A MONTH? GREAT, I CAN LEARN THE BATTING AVERAGE OF EVERY PLAYER EVER!

For this reason, in Step 1 you get the really easy job of taking a break. In all situations except those that are immediately and directly life-threatening, the wisest first choice is to have a rest. By stopping whatever you are doing in relation to your child's behavior, you may have already removed 50 percent of the problem—what you have been doing. Sometimes, by continually trying to solve a problem, we can make it worse. Sitting back and not intervening allows you to look at the problem with refreshed eyes and to consider alternative ways to respond.

Be warned: when a parent decides not to intervene, the problem might escalate temporarily. This may be because the child is so used to your response that they will behave in such a way until they get the response they are looking for.

At some stage during Week 1, go and do something pleasant for yourself. Get more sleep. The next six weeks will require a lot of you, and you need to be fresh and ready to approach this. While you are resting up, use the checklists at the end of Chapters 2–7 and observe your child's patterns closely.

Think about changing the mood of your home. If your house is like that of most bright kids, it can be fairly frantic and chaotic—not the oasis of calm you and your family deserve.

Use some of the mood changers described in Chapter 13 to help you begin the change. Changing your family's diet, increasing the amount of sleep, altering the lighting, being more physically active, and playing music more regularly will send a message to all of your family that "something's up."

> *One mother described her son's reaction at this stage: "I had the music soft and low, the lamps on, and I was lying on the couch reading a magazine when my 16-year-old came in. This was a vast contrast to the usual hurly-burly of family life. His immediate response was, 'What's up with you?' I turned, hugged him, and replied, 'Darling, you're home,' and wandered off. He spent the next few hours warily checking in on me."*

Whatever the age of your child, you need to make a commitment to yourself to *stop telling* and *stop yelling*. If you want to change your family life, you are going to have to begin that change.

There are a number of things parents can do that are likely to optimize bright kids' neurochemistry and improve their moods (see the table at the end of Chapter 12). The aim is for you to calm the torrid seas rather than fueling the fires of battle.

For those of you who have been feeling bailed up and tormented by a bright kid, this is going to sound unfair: if a family is to improve, the first people who are going to have to change what they do are the parents. Let's put this as a golden rule:

Families change only when the parents change what they do.

Parents of bright kids get lots and lots of practice in telling their children to do the right thing. It becomes such a habit that it can be hard for parents to give it up. Even worse, the bright kids themselves are so used to being told (and then reacting against it) that they also don't know what to do when their parents stop telling. It may not be that the things you've been saying are bad or wrong, it's just that the very act of telling and reminding them perpetuates the very behaviors you want to see less of.

During this first step, don't expect too much of your bright kid. Don't get fussed. Access that long-forgotten implacable, calm, carefree you. The aim of the first step is to begin changing the mood of your home.

If usual chores don't get done, quietly and calmly do them yourself, preferably when your child is out of the house. Remember, your aim is to change a whole family pattern—and that's more important than having your child remember to feed the goldfish.

If you feel the situation is too grave or life-threatening to take a break, get some professional assistance either for your child or—if she won't take it—for yourself. Life is too short and too precious for you to be spending it panicking.

As an aside, Manipulator kids will very quickly sense a change in family patterns. This may cause some of them to do things to try to please you. While this can be lovely for any tired, overworked, overwrought parent, be careful not to let them use their helpful behaviors to manipulate you.

Takeaways

- Change yourself and you will go some way towards changing your bright kid's behaviors.
- Stop telling and stop yelling.
- Go easy on yourself so that you can feel rested.
- Think creatively about the changes you want to see.

15

Build belonging—
Step 2

During Step 2 you leap into further inaction. Continue not to intervene. And as you idle away the hours, remember what we said in Chapter 1: *The most powerful factor in your child's path towards a great life is their relationship with you. Having a positive, strong bond with you is the top priority.*

All you have to do in Step 2 is create a feeling of belonging for your bright kid. Belonging is the essence of resilience. It is the most powerful antidote we know of for suicide, violence, and drug abuse. Bright kids need to have loads and loads of resilience, and where they get the strongest dose of it is from you.

Belonging offers a remedy for the fears of childhood—rejection, isolation, and abandonment. Bright kids fear these more than other children.

When family life has been torrid, the sense of belonging in the family often deteriorates. In Step 2 we consider how to build it back up.

Building resilience and belonging in a family requires:

1. a strategy for creating belonging,

2. building a culture of cooperation, and

3. being clear about what you want.

(Points 2 and 3 will be covered in the next chapters.)

Developing a strategy for belonging

On the next few pages is an outline of belonging as it affects the different types of bright kids. Have a look at this and see if any particular issues have priority for you or your child, as these can guide you in setting some clear goals.

Belonging and the characteristics of bright kids

Healthy belonging

Manipulators

Self—can be direct with people and allow others to see their own vulnerabilities.
Family—is able to be a child rather than a mini-parent. Doesn't have to impress all the time.
School—can complain directly that something is unfair rather than being sneaky.
Friends—has some close friends of a similar age.
Communal values—wants to succeed but can make mistakes.

Negotiators

Self—is energetic and focused on achieving positive goals.
Family—is an entertainer who knows when to stop. Is able to express and receive genuine love.
School—finds positive outlets for skills.
Friends—mixes with a range of friends rather than just those with similar inclinations.
Communal values—wheels and deals.

Debaters

Self—is able to meet own needs.
Family—feels loved, wanted, and listened to.
School—is able to consider others' needs and to comply with at least *some* decisions by a teacher without extensive debate.
Friends—is able to take a backseat role at times with friends without feeling mistreated.
Communal values—disputes and debates.

Healthy belonging (continued)

Competitors

Self—is self-reliant but can accept loss and mistakes.
Family—is able to ask others for help as well as assisting others.
School—is successful but not domineering.
Friends—has some stable friends.
Communal values—wants to succeed but can make mistakes; can occasionally tolerate not winning; tries activities that he/she may not be good at.

Dare Devils

Self—cares for own safety; can plan and assess dangers and risks.
Family—can let others know what the plans are.
School—is able to focus on challenges.
Friends—has a diverse range, from thrillseekers to calmer kids.
Communal values—engages in thrills and spills; plans for an exciting, adventurous life.

Passive Resisters

Self—communicates openly.
Family—confides and talks through at least some problems.
School—has a trusting and open relationship with at least one teacher.
Friends—has a few positive confidants.
Communal values—spends time alone but can come out of their shell.

Distorted belonging

Manipulators

Self—needs to impress and to give false impressions.
Family—acts like a mini-adult and can out-parent the parents.
School—is sneaky.
Friends—has generally short-term friendships only.
Communal values—seeks adult approval to the extent of alienating peers. Thinks the end justifies the means.

Negotiators

Self—is ruthless, lacking consideration or compassion.
Family—is dismissive of family requests and rules.
School—decides he/she is not good at school and gives up trying. Attains "success" through being class clown.
Friends—uses affection to gain ground. Employs emotional blackmail.
Communal values—trusts no one.

Distorted belonging (continued)
Debaters   **Self**—can't accept affection; holds grudges for a long, long time.   **Family**—has poor relationships with brothers and sisters.   **School**—wears teachers out through disputes.   **Friends**—apart from fellow combatants, has very few true friends.   **Communal values**—seeks revenge.
Competitors   **Self**—is lonely and isolated.   **Family**—spends a lot of time in their room; doesn't participate in family activities.   **School**—has a "must win at any cost" attitude.   **Friends**—boasts, competes, and gloats; does not win gracefully.   **Communal values**—restricts activities to those he/she is definitely good at.
Dare Devils   **Self**—lacks self-care and consideration for the safety of others.   **Family**—finds it hard to accept affection and love.   **School**—finds it hard to settle and focus in class.   **Friends**—mixes only with other kids with poor impulse control.   **Communal values**—is ruled by impulses.
Passive Resisters   **Self**—is isolated and hard to know.   **Family**—does not participate with or confide in family.   **School**—loses clothes and property; is close to no one.   **Friends**—has either no close friends or a few unsociable ones who stand out from the rest of the peer group.   **Communal values**—withdraws.

Shifting a bright kid's sense of belonging will take some time. First, consider how you can improve your own relationship with him. One father decided to play half an hour of computer games every day with his son. A mother took on the project of letting everyone in her family know that they were loved.

There's an old saying: if you do the same thing you've always done, you'll wind up with the same results you've always had.

Having an extraordinary family begins with you doing something extraordinary to build a great relationship with your bright kid. Think about something your bright kid would enjoy doing with you, and do it. It needs to be something out of the ordinary. Set aside at least 20 minutes of unadulterated "you" time without demands, and do something fun where they take the lead and enjoy having you all to themselves. Here are a few ideas.

Some activities to build belonging

- Cooking together
- Having them teach you a computer game
- Learning a musical instrument
- Exercise
- Watching sports together
- Joining a sports team
- Scouts/ Cubs
- Watching a TV show
- Walking
- Playing cards
- Playing chess, dominoes, backgammon
- Caring for pets
- Camping
- Collecting things

Takeaways

- Belonging is the cornerstone of resilience, and is the most powerful antidote we have to self-harm, violence, and drug abuse.
- Look for areas of distorted belonging in your child.
- Look for opportunities to increase belonging. This will take some time, but it is the bedrock of an improved family.

16

Create a culture of cooperation—Step 3

Parents of bright kids often report feeling that there are times when their family operates on the lowest common denominator. This is surviving, not thriving. Expectations are well and truly lowered. Hopes of an agreeable, cooperative family life have vanished: those wishes have been obliterated by conflict, disagreements, and hostility. This happens to all families from time to time.

> *Mrs. Harmon described her tyrannical daughter, Emily: "We started to live a walking-on-eggshells lifestyle. Any time we asked her to do anything, we would have a full-scale war. Torrents of abuse, stand-over tactics, the whole bit. Eventually it seemed easier not to ask her to do or be involved in anything. After some time we really had as little to do with one another as possible. The family was miserable and she was too."*

Ask for cooperation

Building a culture of cooperation means raising your own expectations about what is possible in your family. The first thing to do is to increase the number of requests made in the family. People can't learn to be cooperative unless you give them opportunities to help out.

Most families with bright kids give up on making many requests. This is understandable: the likely outcome doesn't seem worth the effort. The problem is that this leads to a family atmosphere of sacrifice rather than helpfulness. Requests lead to later, greater cooperation. If you've ever been asked by someone to do something and have done it, you were probably much more likely to assist if they asked you for something else on a second occasion. Bright kids often don't get asked to help people. Their parents and teachers have often given up.

Requests should always be politely asked and can be large or small, such as:

"Sally, could you please pass the salt?"

"Jack, would you please go to the store and get some butter?"

"Lyn, could you please help me by doing this load of laundry?"

WHY DON'T I GIVE YOU A BIG HUG, AND THEN WE CAN TALK ABOUT CLEANING UP MY ROOM?

In families with bright kids, not every request is going to be met with an enthusiastic, "Yes, Mom [or Dad], I'll do it straight away." That's okay.

This is a two-way street that we are going to gradually travel down. Not only will you be making more requests, you're also going to try to say yes more often.

When you get a flat "No way" in response to a request, don't react negatively. Smile sweetly and murmur something like, "Oh well, thanks for considering it," and move on. Don't linger and *don't* get drawn into an argument. Asking them to help out is aimed at eliciting a more positive atmosphere in the home—it is not a reason to go to war!

Demonstrate cooperation

Parents with bright kids often tell me they end up saying "No" to almost everything because they don't know how it will turn out. Try this as an experiment: from No to Yes.

Building a culture of cooperation means that *you* also have to be cooperative. Spend a day saying "Yes" to your bright kid. Whatever he suggests, you agree to! It's simple but scary. He says, "I want to go to a party," you say, "Great idea, I'll get my coat." He says, "I don't want to go to school," you say, "Fantastic, what will we do together?" He says, "I want to fly to Africa," you say, "Great idea, let's work out a way to do that." He says, "I want frog legs and ice cream for dinner," you say, "Excellent, I'll get the ice cream, you find the frogs."

Get the idea? You'll agree to do almost anything with them. Probably by the end of the day, they will be so sick of you being so damn agreeable, they'll either think you're on drugs or start seriously wondering whether you are insane. It takes that sort of determination to shift a family from grumpy coercion to something resembling willing compliance.

Secondly, show them the behaviors you want to see more of. Kids do what they see other people do. Bright kids are especially sensitive to the environment around them. If you want them to be calm and settled, you will need to become calm and settled yourself. To repeat something from the first chapter, two crocodile brains equals a lot of snapping!

This means you are no longer playing by their rules. This can confuse many bright kids. They've had years of battle-hardening experience. They know what to do when you get angry or defensive. If they start haranguing, arguing, disputing, debating, or insulting you, say, "I'll give you two minutes to see if you can get yourself together. If you can't speak about this calmly, I'll leave and you can come back to me when you are calmer." If they are still fuming, leave. There is nothing to be gained by gritting your teeth and putting up with their bad behavior—and much to be lost.

Some families find it worthwhile having a code word or a physical gesture that indicates, "Let's take a break from this discussion for ten minutes."

Building a culture of cooperation with the different types of bright kids

You need to know your young person's style so that you can start building a positive family culture.

Manipulators

As Manipulators are often keen to impress adults, superficial cooperation is easy to attain. Genuine cooperation may take a little longer. Praise them for their helpfulness but stay close. For six weeks we want them to have no chance to engage in sneaky or underhand behaviors.

Negotiators

Negotiators can be difficult to encourage towards cooperation. Their "What's in it for me?" attitude can mislead you into trying to force them to do things. Resist this. For six weeks you are going to show them it is preferable to be a collaborator than a Negotiator. Pick one or, at most, two areas and build cooperation in those areas. Clearly make requests, raise your expectations, and don't waver.

Debaters

Ah, the unfairness of it all! Debaters are so used to tallying who does what and when and who got the biggest share that true cooperation is a foreign language to them. This will take a concerted effort on your part by being extremely helpful to them for no good reason. Once you have shown them how to cooperate for some time, you can start making small (and tentative) requests.

Competitors

Cooperation is an anathema to Competitors. While you won't shift their competitive spirit, you can show them there is a more collaborative way to win. Involving them in community service projects where they receive recognition for good deeds is one way. In the home, give them some responsibility that involves helping others.

Dare Devils

Dare Devils aren't just reckless, they are also often kind hearted. Requests that have a sense of urgency often involve them best. This is especially the case if there is a sense of challenge. For example, "I'm just about to serve dinner. Would you mind quickly feeding the goldfish?"

Passive Resisters

With cooperation comes social interaction—something some Passive Resisters want to avoid. Requesting that they care for younger children or animals is a good place to start. You'll have to be clear that you won't accept the stock response, "I'll do it later." Persist with requests and praise their efforts. Bringing these kids out of their shell sets them up for life.

Magical mystery tours

Another way of building a culture of cooperation is to shake up the routines of family life. The following strategy has been used successfully with countless families, and has been so successful that I recommend you consider doing it at least one day each year for each of your children.

Here's what it involves: invite your bright kid to come and do things with you. Don't tell her what you're inviting her to do in advance, just say, "I'd like you to come out with me today, there's a few things I've got to do."

If it's a school day, so much the better. Take her out of your local area to lunch or to the movies, the art gallery, a music event, to church, or to test-drive new cars that you have no intention of buying. Take her to places you normally wouldn't go with her. If she whines and complains and tells you it's boring, just agree and smile pleasantly.

Throughout the day, keep shifting from event to event. If she complains about one event, just say, "Oh don't worry, we're not there yet," and imply there is more to come. If she whines and says, "I want to go home," either reply by saying, "Just a little while longer" or, if she is seriously complaining, offer to return her to school.

The reason for this "magical mystery tour" is that bright kids are very accustomed to controlling their world. Spontaneity doesn't feature highly on their list of experiences. Broadening their experience gives them another view of your life as well as showing them that the world is bigger than they can imagine.

If your bright kid is prone to perfectionism—she *has* to get things right and things *have* to be just so—this strategy should be used more often.

Spontaneity is the antidote to controlling, perfectionist behavior.

The idea is to expose your bright kid to a different view of the world. The idea is not to give her a day where she necessarily does all her favorite things. It's not a day spent doting on her. Even so, it's a good idea to have a few treats mixed in with other experiences, just in case the complaints get too exasperating.

Bright kids who are used to lots of control don't give up their power too easily. Even so, the magical mystery tour teaches them that life can be adventurous.

Takeaways

A culture of cooperation:
- doesn't occur by accident in families—you have to create it, and
- is built when you start asking for help, demonstrating cooperation yourself, and developing a spirit of helpfulness in all family members.

17

Start a new dance—Step 4

Getting what you want requires planning for what you want. Starting a new dance involves thinking about the changes you really want for yourself and for your bright kid.

Be clear about what you want

Write down in three sentences or less what your goal is (see page 121). Make it one goal only. Be careful: it is often easier to write down what you don't want rather than what you do. For example, "I want him to stop running off from school" or "I want her to stop teasing her younger brother" should be changed into the positive, "I want him to attend school" or "I want her to learn to be civil towards her brother."

Goals should be short, precise, and phrased in terms of starting something rather than stopping something. Look over your goal. Is there any way of making it smaller or more achievable? The larger a goal, the easier it is to miss. Break it down if at all possible. List all the things you've already tried that haven't worked. This will remind you not to use them again.

Negotiators (a.k.a. "the Barts") are so skilled at shifting the battle to suit themselves, they can run rings around you. Fewer goals are better. One or, at most, two goals every six weeks is the most parents can cope with. Remember the fable of the race between the plodding tortoise and the speedy hare? The tortoise won by being persistent. Be the tortoise!

In Step 4, start observing your bright kid. Your quest is to find times when the problem doesn't happen. Don't pay attention or respond when the problem happens—you already know enough about the problem. The more puzzling issue is to find out what's going on when the problem *isn't* around. If we can work out what *is* happening when the problem behaviors are *not*, we are well on our way to an answer.

For example, what's happening when he seems happier? What is going on when he is calm and friendly, or when he does come out of his room to talk?

Most parents, when they are first asked to notice when the problem behavior is not happening, either shrug and say, "Easy, it's when he is getting his own way," or laugh and say, "Hey, the kid has to sleep some time." It's important to have a fresh look at this.

For almost every bright kid I have ever worked with, there have been many factors that lead to problem and non-problem behaviors happening. You might like to photocopy the next page and use it for a week or so to see what you discover.

Keep non-problem times firmly in your sights. It's too easy to get sucked back into thinking about the problem and whatever it is that might be causing it. This only blinds you to opportunities for change. If you find things that seem to be happening when the problem isn't, see if you can make more of those things happen more often.

Takeaways

- If you keep doing what you've always done, you'll end up with the same outcomes.
- Set some clear, unambiguous goals.
- Spy on your bright kid to find "non-problem times."

Bright kids—Starting a new dance

Your goal (what you want to see more of):

Problem behavior (what you want to see less of):

Day	Problem-free times	What was happening
Sunday		
Monday		
Tuesday		
Wednesday		
Thursday		
Friday		
Saturday		

18

The dance—
Step 5

For thousands of years, the main levers for change that parents have had are fear, bribery, and distraction. These still work in many families today but they don't work well with bright kids.

Bright kids "pay it back and then some." If you give them anger, they give you more anger, with a twist. Bribe them, and you'll find that even the most basic household task has an extravagant cost. Try to dominate and control, and they either openly defy you or else get sneaky and use "rat cunning."

In families with bright kids, we need to shift the main levers of change from fear, bribery, and distraction to praise, habit, and motivation. There is a lovely Zen teaching paradox (or *koan*) that sums up this type of parenting. It is:

> *Hold on tight with an open hand.*

Hold on tight with an open hand? What this means for parenting bright kids is guiding them without controlling them; using your power to shape family routines and habits without descending into conflict and dismay. This doesn't mean you need:

- the patience of Nelson Mandela,
- the determination of Napoleon Bonaparte,

- the caring concern of Florence Nightingale,
- the wisdom of Solomon,
- the love of Mother Teresa, combined with
- the strategic planning of Genghis Khan.

What you need are *rituals.*

Rituals

Rituals are family acts that occur regardless of the vagaries of life. Together with belonging, they are the very foundation of resilience for bright kids. Rituals can be as commonplace as the Sunday roast, the walk after dinner, the movies on Tuesday night, or the visit to Grandma's each week. They can be exciting or so regular that they become dull. The power of rituals for bright kids is that they deliver an unambiguous message: *this is the way we do things here.*

Rituals do not require discussion and debate. They are not open for negotiation. They are regular events that parents decide on and make happen. Rituals are the rocks that the river of family life flows around.

Families do not work well as democracies; they work best as benevolent dictatorships. Kids do not have to be consulted about family rituals. Parents can decide on the rituals they want and implement them.

Most families, when they get a bit ragged and frayed, find they need to put new rituals into place. While rituals can be about having a pleasant time, they can also be about the necessary efficiencies of life.

Let's talk about three types of ritual in areas that are often issues for families with bright kids:

1. getting out of the house on a weekday,
2. household cleanliness, and
3. spending some time together.

1. Getting out of the house on a weekday

*To get the kids to school on time, we need to leave the house
at 8 a.m. sharp. It's now 7:30 a.m. A battle is raging in
the bathroom. One of my kids has slept in, another one has
finished breakfast and is complaining about the others.
My levels of cortisol and adrenaline have reached all-time
peaks, when one of the kids says she needs a special hat for an
activity. The cat has reacted to all the energy in the house
and has just vomited on the rug.*

Sound familiar in any way?

Across the country, in homes everywhere, a dramatic soap
opera is played out every morning. Tricky behaviors can be at
their peak when the clock is ticking and the pressure is on. The
classic error is trying to do too much in too little time.

*One mother told me she was sick and tired of the war zone
that occurred in her house every morning. By 9 a.m. every
morning she felt like reaching for a major tranquilizer or
something stronger. Her solution, which may be a bit too
drastic for you, was to shift her entire time schedule. Rather
than waking at 6:30 a.m. and fighting tooth-and-nail to be
out of the house on time, she decided to make breakfast the
main family meal of the day.*

*"I read somewhere that you should eat breakfast like a
king, lunch like a prince, and have your evening meal like
a pauper," she told me. "So I decided to reinvent our life.
I'm up at 4:30 a.m. and I cook the best damn breakfast you
have ever seen. The level of hunger from having a very light
evening meal plus the delicious aromas wafting through the
house entrance even the laziest pair of nostrils. By 7 a.m.
we sit down together for the main meal of the day. To do
this, we all need to be washed. Whereas we used to talk
about how the day had gone, now we talk about our plans
for the day."*

Now you may not want to go as far as that mother did, but there are a few great ideas that I got from her that I regularly suggest to families with bright kids:

- **Make sure your bright kid(s) and you get adequate sleep.** Decide on the best time for the family to wake up, and start shifting the start of the day to that time. It may take you a few weeks to get there. That's fine. Focus more on the time people awaken rather than on bedtime. Once a wake-up time is firmly established, you can then put your energies into enforcing a bedtime.

- **Cook a great breakfast.** Not only will your bright kid's mood improve, she will find it easier to concentrate in school. A condition of sitting down to breakfast is being washed and dressed. Parents of bright kids often respond to this idea by saying that their child is not hungry in the morning. Try reducing food intake in the evening and see what happens.

- **Play music to wake people up.** Half an hour before you expect people to be up, put on your favorite songs for the day. Play them loud. Sing along. One father who tried this told me his teenage son would get up just to turn his music off.

- **Allow enough time.** You simply can't mobilize bright kids in a short period of time. Sure, you can lay down challenges to the Competitors and the Dare Devils, reward the Debaters, cajole the Passive Resisters, praise the Manipulators, and wheel and deal with the Negotiators, but you don't want to do it every morning.

In one of my previous books, *Raising Real People*, I cited a survey of parents on the top 10 things they did to get kids out of bed in the morning. Let me repeat them here.

The top 10 ways parents get kids out of bed

1. Play your old CDs at full volume.
2. Invite their friends over for breakfast.
3. Get a dog to jump on their bed.
4. Get a larger or scarier animal to jump on their bed.

5. Scream "Get up" into a tape recorder, and make a continuous loop of the tape. Place the tape recorder outside their bedroom door and then creep off.

6. Have the family breakfast in their room.

7. Sneak into their bedroom and change the clock so it appears to be hours later than it actually is. Parents say this is a one-time event, but it's such good fun it's worth doing.

8. Have a morning phone call. If they have a cell phone, call it. As you will have wisely banned cell phones from bedrooms, they just may get up to answer it.

9. Come into their room and start an interesting conversation about anything, and don't stop until they get up.

10. Hop into bed with them and have a cuddle. Be warned, though: one mother who did this nodded off back to sleep and was late for work.

2. Household cleanliness

Household cleanliness may not be the biggest, most panicky issue that you have with your bright kid, but in surveys of parents it regularly comes up as one of the biggest issues facing parents on a day-to-day basis.

We can all admire the cavalier attitude of the mother who told me her strategy for dealing with messy bedrooms:

1. Clean up the room. Make it impeccable. Make it delightful.

2. Take a photo of the bedroom.

3. Take the film out of the camera and take it to someone who can blow up the photo to poster-size.

4. Bring the poster home.

5. Close the bedroom door.

6. Stick the poster on the door.

7. Pretend that is what it looks like.

Rituals around household cleanliness need to be handled carefully with bright kids. Even the most fair-minded parent—after meticulously preparing a cleaning roster—will find the Debaters complaining it's unfair, the Manipulators angling for special privileges, and the Competitors challenging you to come up with a consequence so severe that they will actually participate in the whole process. Having discussed this issue with tens of thousands of families, I have come to the conclusion that there is only one really viable solution. No, it's not to give in and hire a cleaning firm. It is *the clean-up hour.*

Most families of bright kids find that the easiest way to arrange clean-up times is to have an hour each week when everyone pitches in and does whatever is needed to make the house look respectable. One family who tried this made it into a real occasion, with people taking turns to pick the music to clean to, and following the clean-up time with a special brunch or lunch. For bright kids, this has the advantage of delivering a message that a family is a unit where everyone helps everyone out and everyone participates.

3. Spending some time together

These are the most important rituals of all because they build belonging. Belonging underpins resilience, and giving your bright kid the ability to overcome adversity is a gift that sets him up for life. You may already belong to a cultural or religious group that has weekly rituals. It is still worth developing a few family rituals which occur regardless of how people are behaving or what has recently occurred.

In talking to many bright kids who have since developed into positive adults, I often ask them what they think helped them to grow up and succeed as well as they have. They often talk about being loved and supported, and when I ask them what helped them to feel loved, they will almost invariably mention a ritual that occurred in their family. Rituals act like coat hangers for people to hang the good memories of their childhood on.

It is worth thinking about two types of rituals you can have:

1. *Family rituals*, such as dinner together, a family walk, playing a game on Monday evening, watching a particular TV show together. Select something that everyone can participate in and will enjoy. It doesn't need to be expensive; the best rituals often cost nothing.

2. *One-on-one rituals*. As bright kids often compete for attention in fairly counter-productive ways, having one-on-one time with you can ease their negative behaviors. Think of one thing you and your bright kid could do together each week that would involve nobody else and do it. If you are a single parent with a few children, I suggest you rotate your children's special rituals, get some support and look for ways to do this. It builds positive relationships.

Takeaways

Creating new behaviors in bright kids involves:
- being clear about what changes you want,
- noticing what *is* going on when the problem is *not*, and
- creating new family rituals and ways of relating.

Part Four

POSITIVE
LIFE HABITS

L ife is a dance. Each of us creates our own rhythm and steps. Bright kids are often fiercely independent and strong-willed. They will certainly weave their own magic.

The power of parents to shape the lives of bright kids is considerable. Most bright kids I've worked with do, in the long term, follow family patterns and habits that were set up by their parents.

In the following chapters, we'll discuss how to parent powerfully in order to create the life skills your bright kid will need to succeed.

19

Thriving in the age of anxiety

In the Western world, much of childhood has become an indoor game. It is no longer the bruised-knee, bat-and-ball, hurtling-around-the-local-park game of a generation ago. Children interact electronically, multi-task, and have ways of inter-connecting that are beyond the scrutiny and sometimes even the awareness of parents.

Tempting as it is sometimes to turn off the electronics, the computers, and the televisions, I think there are better ways to prepare your children to thrive in the future. In a world that has so much to offer children, it is essential to work out what is of benefit.

The current generation of young people is in many ways the most well-informed, privileged, and protected group of young people in history, yet they seem to derive little satisfaction or inspiration from it.

To misquote P.G. Wodehouse, while they are not exactly disgruntled, it is fair to say that they are far from "gruntled."

Their generation

In focus groups, I ask young people to describe their generation. This is what they regularly say.

- Little respect for elders
- Reliant on technology
- Indecisive
- Self-absorbed
- Short-term view
- Less trusting
- More active
- Less mature
- Loose morality
- More pressure to grow up quickly
- More parental freedom
- Greater financial independence
- Higher expectations on us
- Reliant on friends more than family
- More options for help
- Takes advantage of others
- Less religious
- More tolerant of differences
- More adaptable
- Not very responsible
- Knows it all
- Excessive social life
- Lazy
- Less committed
- World's become small and there is nothing that hasn't been explored.

Not a very flattering self-portrait, is it?

While some of these trends may be developmental and may change as teenagers grow, several themes are consistent:

- their reliance on external stimulation for challenges,
- their brevity of attention and concentration,
- their requirement of immediate outcomes to motivate them,
- their distrust of strangers and public institutions,
- they are information-rich but experience-poor, and
- they are "just-in-time" learners. For example, they might say, "Why should I learn that now when I can download it from the Web later on?"

Now you may think, haven't adults been complaining about younger generations in this way since time immemorial? You may well be right, but I think there is now an added twist: many young people are growing up in a world of fear and anxiety. Uncertainty about world safety definitely resonates with them. The fact that they have grown up in a world that emphasizes information but doesn't value experience highly helps to amplify this.

The young people most likely to be negatively affected by this wave of anxiety are bright kids. Bright kids are reactive: they react to being told to do things, to parental requests or demands, to anger and conflicts. Whatever is going around, they can react to. The life skills covered in this Part help bright kids to dance their own dance rather than marching to the drum-beat of others.

Are bright kids worriers?

With all the bluster and determination that bright kids have, it can be easy to miss the fact that many of them are anxious. In fact, their anger is often a disguise for anxiety.

About one in three kids habitually worries. Worry in a Dare Devil kid may not be a bad thing, but if there's too much worry, these kids won't try out new behaviors, or they'll give up and won't attempt anything they think might be difficult.

Forceful kids are often very sensitive to where they are in the pecking order of life. Constantly assessing where you are in relation to others destroys self-esteem and builds jealousy and a fear of failure. This type of measuring can lead to self-absorption, alienation and isolation.

What do they worry about?

What kids worry about changes as they grow up. Little kids worry about monsters, supernatural creatures, and separation from their parents. Early primary-school-age kids worry about safety and sometimes their ability to do well at school. Later in primary school, the worries shift to the peer group. In the teenage years, schoolwork is a major source of worry for many young people.

Separation anxiety

If a child asked you, "Will you be coming back home today?" I guess an honest answer would be, "There is a 99.9 percent probability that I will return, but if some awful accident happens …." No one would alarm a child by giving this type of answer. Kids need to feel safe and secure that their parent(s) will be there for them and continue to be so.

Some kids worry about being separated from their parents. In some cases this means they don't want to go to school, and attach themselves to a parent. As early as possible in this process, it is worth thinking, "How do I help my child feel secure that I am staying around?"

Parents of bright kids worry, too!

Will they fit in, grow up, succeed at school, find a friend, have a meaningful relationship, be able to let others win … The list of worries for parents of forceful kids is endless.

Especially since the terrorist attacks of 2001, I have observed an increase in anxiety among young people. This has been demonstrated by their reluctance to try out unknown activities, to risk meeting new friends, and to have a go at school in areas where they might fail.

For bright kids to thrive in life, they need to play to their strengths. One of those strengths is boldness. Being bold, clear, and direct when you live in cautious and anxious times is one avenue towards success. Use the great leadership traits of your bright kid to give him an advantage.

This new wave of anxiety that besets much of the Western world is exacerbated by a perception that success is a limited commodity. If you begin to subscribe to this point of view, this fear becomes contagious as you go into "overload." Your bright kid may begin to believe that success is unattainable.

For parents of bright kids, there is often much else to worry about. These kids often don't get the best school reports, aren't the easiest to settle, aren't always on their best behavior when you want them to be, and aren't always the most popular with other adults.

Believe in your bright kid. He has the drive and the get-up-and-go to change the world if he wants to.

Why we live with increased anxiety

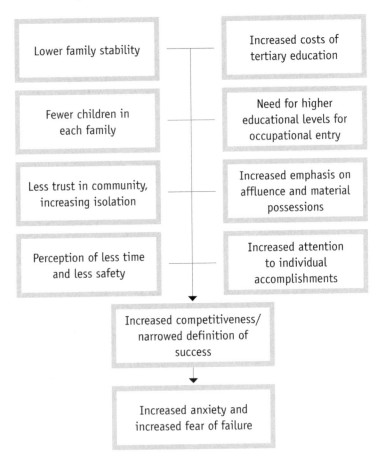

Lower family stability	Increased costs of tertiary education
Fewer children in each family	Need for higher educational levels for occupational entry
Less trust in community, increasing isolation	Increased emphasis on affluence and material possessions
Perception of less time and less safety	Increased attention to individual accomplishments

Increased competitiveness/ narrowed definition of success

Increased anxiety and increased fear of failure

Takeaways

- We live in anxious times.
- Bright kids are often worriers, but their behavior can mask this.
- Talk positively about life and what the world has to offer.
- Model a positive outlook towards the future.

20
Self-esteem skills

S ome bright kids have a great talent for bringing out the worst in some people. As a result, their self-esteem can take a bit of a battering. Others build strong self-esteem on flimsy grounds: the Competitors do this by being the best, the Manipulators by impressing adults, and the Negotiators by outwitting others.

Parents of bright kids need to develop their children's self-esteem.

The person you speak most to is yourself, so help bright kids to think positively about their lives. One way of doing this is to introduce into your family the concept of "dolphin" and "shark" thoughts. "Dolphin" thoughts are those thoughts that are helpful, while "shark" thoughts can eat you up. When you catch bright kids expressing shark thoughts, stop them and make them tell you several dolphin thoughts as well.

Go on a treasure hunt!

Go on a search to find the talents, skills, contributions, abilities, and interests that your bright kid has. Ask her about them. Make much of them. Praise them.

Families that work well seem to praise one another a lot. Compliments are given, positive efforts are commented on. Optimism is in the air. But even in these families, bright kids still shrug and say, "Yeah Mom" or "Yeah Dad" when they receive a compliment.

Teaching the skills of self-praise is very useful. One way of doing this is to ask questions about *any* achievement or accomplishment, such as:

"How did you do that?"

"How come you did so well at that test?"

"What did you do?" and

"Have you been doing homework behind my back?"

At first they will think you are accusing them of cheating, so tell them you're not. These questions force them to account for their successes, and by providing answers to you, they can learn to praise themselves.

When all of the praise comes from you, they can easily dismiss it. But when they have to explain their own achievements, they must do so in their own words—and when they do so in their own words, *they* own the praise and become fully aware of it.

These skills are also important for performance at school. High self-esteem students attribute their successes to their own efforts, while those who are not resilient often attribute their successes to luck or chance. Because of their sometimes highly competitive natures—especially the Debaters ("Maggies"), the Manipulators ("Angelicas"), and the Competitors ("Winstons")—these children often denigrate the successes they do have.

Self-esteem is not only about learning how to acknowledge when you have done something well, but also how to set in place strategies to improve your performance next time. Families who foster self-esteem certainly celebrate achievements and successes, but it doesn't stop there. The parents in these families may ask their children:

- how well they would like to do next time,
- how they plan to do as well as they would like to,
- what it will take to get that kind of result, and
- how they would feel if they actually managed to achieve that.

One of the keys to having high self-esteem is to have a skill, a talent, or an ability identified in the late childhood/early teenage years and for parents to make a bit of a fuss over this skill. This is particularly powerful if it fits in with an interest of the young person's and if she can be encouraged to set goals to improve that skill even further. Success in a part-time job can also be valuable in building self-esteem during middle adolescence.

> *"No one can make you feel inferior without your consent."*
> Eleanor Roosevelt

The language of optimism

Families, when they work well, also teach children the skills of optimism. This is the ability to explain successes in such a way that they are caused by the person, reflect ongoing abilities in that person, and are linked to other strengths the person has. Basically, optimists take credit for the things that go right in their lives and tend to shrug off negative events as the result of external factors such as luck, fate, or other people. Pessimists blame themselves for what goes wrong and explain most positive events as the result of external forces.

For example, if a young person succeeds in getting a good grade for a piece of work, it could be explained optimistically as: "I really used effort and imagination to get that mark, and I guess I am pretty good at school after all." Whereas a pessimistic way of explaining the same event

WHAT COULD POSSIBLY GO WRONG?

would be: "It was good luck that the teacher was in a good mood when she graded the essay and that she missed some of the errors I made."

In the optimistic explanation, the cause of the high grade is due to the young person's own ability, which is seen as a permanent part of his character, and so may apply in other settings. The pessimistic statement explains away the success as being outside the person's control, due to temporary circumstances such as luck and the teacher's mood, and so may occur only in this situation.

Similarly, if dealing with a setback such as failing to play a musical piece well:

- **Optimistically:** "I haven't had the time that I need to put into practicing to play that piece well, and I will put more time into it before trying again."

- **Pessimistically:** "I can't play the guitar," "I'm tone deaf," or "I'm stupid."

In the optimistic statement, the setback is explained as temporary and changeable, whereas in the pessimistic statement it is seen as being due to a permanent, enduring failing on the part of the person.

The way that parents explain the successes and setbacks in their own lives can strongly influence whether their children develop more optimism or pessimism. And while optimists can sometimes be a little blind to their own shortcomings, this is far preferable to the other option. Optimism is a skill that *can* be taught.

Takeaways

- Success and self-esteem are contagious.
- Go on a treasure hunt for gems within yourself and within your bright kid.
- Bright kids have great attributes that often get overlooked.
- Develop the habit of optimism.

21

Self-awareness and awareness of others

Bright kids are often a bit of a mystery to themselves. Gung-ho, active people don't easily take the time to reflect and consider their feelings, thoughts, or the deeper parts of their internal world.

Parents of bright kids give them the words through which to see life. This is why the way that you speak about the world is vital to bright kids. It sounds paradoxical, doesn't it? The same kid who will fight you tooth-and-nail over bedtime or will dispute and debate some minor issue for hours also relies on your words to help her understand the world.

A father complained to me that his bright son wasn't motivated at school and seemed reluctant to try things out. I asked the father to listen to himself for a week, to listen to the way he talked about the world. When he came back, the father said he'd noticed that he would walk in the front door, complain that he'd had a dreadful day, that work was tiring, that you couldn't trust those fools, and that nobody listened to good ideas anyway, so what was the point ... He chuckled with the recognition that the person who was teaching his son to be reluctant and unmotivated was himself.

The self-awareness skills

The three major skills of self-awareness are:

1. Recognizing and naming our feelings,
2. Knowing what to do with feelings once you have recognized them, and
3. Changing how we feel about things.

Let's look at each in turn.

1. Recognizing and naming our feelings

I was listening to a Science student talk about thermostats one day, and I thought, wouldn't it be great to have one of those for feelings? Some families place a "Feelings" sign on every family member's bedroom door, and everyone uses theirs to indicate how they are feeling—not a bad idea at all.

You can ask most kids to pause and think about their feelings for a moment, and they'll be able to say something like, "I'm feeling angry." Bright kids aren't good at this. Help them to identify their feelings by saying things like, "It looks to me like you might be worrying about something, is that right?" or "I can't tell from your face if you're feeling annoyed or sad, do you know?" One way of reading the emotions of your bright kid is to notice your own feelings and use these in discussions. For example, "Right now I'm feeling angry. Are you feeling that too?" The skill of recognizing your own feelings helps you decide what is and isn't important. If you don't develop this skill, you can end up reacting to everyone around you without knowing why.

Bright kids who are not tuned in to their own feelings can behave in ways that confuse them. Teach them to track backwards to work out where a particular feeling comes from. It is usually best to do this at the end of the day. For example, "This morning, when we were rushing to get to school and you got upset, what do you think caused you to be upset?" Try not to let your bright kid brush you off with a cursory "Dunno." Be like a detective: "Did you feel upset as soon as you woke up, or after breakfast? Was it when you entered the kitchen or before?"

I know this sounds laborious, but bright kids tend to see the external world as the source of all their feelings. The long-term outcome of this is blaming everyone else every time you feel bad and never taking responsibility for changing the way you feel.

Once bright kids are reasonably able to describe their own feelings, help them to also become aware of the intensity of the feeling by rating it out of 10, where 1 equals feeling it to a small extent and 10 equals feeling it a lot. With very physical kids, like Dare Devils, it can also help to ask them where in their body they feel angry/sad/worried/annoyed.

2. Knowing what to do with feelings once you have recognized them

Try to get bright kids to talk about their feelings. Listen to them carefully and only ask questions that will help them to expand on their feelings. For example:

> **Parent:** *"You look like you are feeling angry. Is that right?"*
> **Bright kid:** *"It's not fair."*
> **Parent:** *"Does that mean you are feeling angry?"*
> **Bright kid:** *"S'pose so. You always pick on me!"*
> **Parent:** *"When did you begin feeling angry?"*
> **Bright kid:** *"I wanted to watch TV."*
> **Parent:** *"So you got angry when I said you couldn't watch TV?"*
> **Bright kid:** *"Everybody else gets to watch what they want."*

This discussion may feel like it is going around in circles, but in fact it is serving a very useful purpose. You might notice the parent doesn't ask the child why he is feeling angry, and doesn't try to explain the reasons for not letting the child watch television. As far as possible, the parent steers the discussion towards the feeling. Talking about feelings allows them to be expressed and increases the chance that they will be resolved. Talking about feelings role-models to the child that there is another way to express anger rather than lashing out or storming off.

Parents of bright kids can feel railroaded into trying to solve problems quickly. Instead, these types of discussions aim to help bright kids learn more about their feelings and be able to talk about them. Offering solutions would either tumble the conversation into an argument or cut it off altogether.

3. Changing how we feel about things

Most bad feelings are not solved or fixed, they are simply outgrown. It is likely, for example, that the things that worried you last week are not the same things you are worrying about now. Life moves on. People get over things. Feelings pass.

There are times, however, when it is useful to change the way we are feeling. There are two main ways to do this. The first involves changing our thinking about an event. This can be as simple as saying, "Oh well, it's not so bad" or "I'll focus on what I have to be grateful for"—that is, swapping shark thoughts for dolphin thoughts.

A father told me his daughter was a Manipulator, and that conflict was ongoing. He decided he would allow himself 10 small conflictual discussions with his daughter each day. When the first one happened (as it inevitably did), he remained calm by thinking to himself, "One down, only nine to go."

The second way of changing feelings is to focus on them. Observing yourself feeling whatever it is you are feeling without interruption often changes that feeling. So sit somewhere quiet and focus on how you are feeling—angry/annoyed/sad/worried. This can help to lift that negative feeling. You can assist bright kids to learn this by asking them to sit quietly for 10 minutes and to focus on their feeling before discussing it with them. I often recommend parents read one of W. Timothy Gallway's *Inner Game* books to help them understand this process.

Awareness of the feelings of others

Being aware of their own feelings significantly advantages bright kids. And being able to read and be aware of the feelings of *others* provides their lives with an enormous boost.

Parents of bright kids can help them learn an awareness of others' feelings by playing "detective games" with their kids. When you are with your child, occasionally point to people in the street and ask, "What do you think that man is feeling?" or "What sort of day do you think that woman is having?" Television shows, movies, pictures of people in magazines, and so on can all be used to help bright kids learn to read the feelings of others.

Talking about the day's events over dinner helps children to understand the positions and perspectives of others. By hearing that one person had a great day while someone else had an awful time helps a child to have compassion.

Several families I have worked with have been interested in becoming more aware of how they argue. To do this, they have drawn a plan of their house, placed it on the fridge door, and recorded the location and time of every argument that occurred over a week. This is a great way to increase everyone's awareness of what's happening in the home.

Takeaways

- Parents give bright kids a way to view themselves and their world.
- Help them to slow down and reflect a bit.
- Help them to become aware of their own feelings.
- Being able to read other people's emotions is a vital survival skill for bright kids.

22

Emotional wellbeing

Growing brains thrive best in stimulating and calm surroundings. But with bright kids, anger, conflict, screaming, and drama are often present by the bucket-load in their families.

Dealing with anger

People who generally can't contain their anger will quickly lose friends.

Teaching children how to control their negative feelings is not easy, but it is essential if they are to have a fulfilling life. Learning that there is someone stronger than your negative emotion or tantrum is a lesson that should be learned at home. If a child learns that his parents are going to give in every time he gets angry, he will use anger to get what he wants. Do you want your child to learn this?

"Hot heads" and "cold hearts"

Children express anger mainly in two ways: with "hot heads" or with "cold hearts."

The "hot heads" show anger very quickly, and need to learn how to control their impulses. They don't hold back, but once it's over, it's over.

Hot heads need to learn how to settle themselves down. They are a bit like a car with great acceleration but very poor brakes: they know a lot about revving-up but a lot less about calming themselves down. This can be done by discussing anger with them, the things they are angry about, and suggesting alternative ways of dealing with those feelings. Younger "hot heads" can be held, gently but firmly, during a tantrum until they calm down. (A warning for parents, though: once you decide to hold them, you need to keep holding them until they really have calmed down, and that can take quite a while!)

The "cold hearts" have more impulse control than the hot heads and are more calculating in the way they express anger. It is almost as if they are saying, "I'll wait till it's really embarrassing before showing my anger." The supermarket aisles are full of cold-heart children sitting down and threatening to scream until you give in. The earlier these cold hearts learn that anger is not an appropriate way to gain attention or privileges, the better. (Another warning for parents: when you take a firm stand and decide not to give in to these children, they get worse, much worse, for a while before they get better.)

Meltdowns and calm-downs

Bright kids can sweep you up in a maelstrom of drama very quickly. Unless you plan carefully, you can find yourself in the eye of a storm, fighting tooth-and-nail for something you don't even care very much about.

Parents of bright kids need to know whether they are dealing with a *meltdown* or a *calm-down* situation.

Meltdowns

Meltdowns occur when there is no way of shifting a bright kid's behavior just by using words. The intensity of the conflict has reached such a point that rational discussion is not possible. As I mentioned earlier, crocodile brains are snapping.

Some indicators that you are in meltdown are:

- The argument has shifted from one area to another in a fairly random way.
- The emphasis seems to be more on expressing anger or frustration than on solving a problem.

■ Someone feels unsafe (this might be you or your bright kid).

■ There has been an act or a threat of physical violence.

In meltdown situations the main aim is to keep people safe. Problems can be sorted out later.

Try to plan your meltdown procedure in advance. In a meltdown, your positioning is important, as is your knowledge of the bright kid. Some bright kids, when they hit a meltdown, need as much space and privacy as you can give them. Leaving them alone, sending them to their room, or walking away—i.e., increasing the physical distance between yourself and them—are some strategies. Other bright kids respond very badly to being left alone. Some become destructive either towards themselves, property, or others. You'll know this from your experience of your bright kid. Obviously, leaving very young bright kids alone when they are angry and distressed is inadvisable. Young bright kids will need someone around who can quietly keep an eye on them as they go through their meltdown.

Meltdown procedures are based on the fact that no one can stay in a rage forever, but while a bright kid is in that furious state, any provocation or intervention *of any kind* will be ineffective. The aim is to keep you and your bright kid safe and allow the situation to cool.

As a general rule, don't position yourself between a raging bright kid and his means of escape, as he may well barrel his way through you to get out. This means staying out of the pathway he has to doors or open windows. Make sure you give a bright kid in meltdown enough space so that you don't get hurt yourself.

In a meltdown, the fewer words you use, the better. If you do have to speak, do so softly and with calm authority. Meltdowns allow you to show bright kids that no matter how angry or out of control they get, you will be able to keep them safe.

A meltdown takes as long as a meltdown takes. There is no way of rushing it. When things are really serious, you have to be prepared to miss that appointment, be late for work, or not walk out the door. Trying to speed up a meltdown will only extend it. Meltdowns will, hopefully, be reasonably rare.

Bright kids often feel quite upset and exhausted after a melt-down, so avoid the temptation to discuss the issues that led to it. Just be with your bright kid and use this time as an opportunity to have him know that you love him.

Calm-downs

Most bright kids need advanced calm-down skills from time to time. The skills of calming down from an upset can be learned and practiced. If you've ever been with someone who is really stressed and irritated, and then walked away feeling a bit jumpy yourself, you'll know that agitation is contagious. The good news is that calmness is also contagious.

In parenting bright kids, there will be times when the most important thing you can do is become self-aware. When a bright kid is all revved-up with nowhere to go, it is all too easy to join him in a chaotic "loop the loop." Instead, pause. Look inside yourself and notice what is happening to you. Is your heart beating faster? Are you breathing quickly? Are you speaking a million words a minute? Pause. Slow down your breathing and lessen the numbers of words you are speaking. Breathe more deeply and slowly between your statements. Change the tone of your voice. Shift your posture so you can be more relaxed. The trick here is to take your sail out of their winds.

When you are in the midst of conflict, you lose perspective. Where you can, slow down, regain your own calm, and then show your bright kid how to decelerate the argument.

Calming bright kids down

Here are some of my favorite methods for calming bright kids down. You might like to read over them and try them out to see which ones suit your child. Teach these methods to bright kids when they are calm so they can use them when they are upset.

The inner bubble of laughter

Close your eyes and gently begin to focus on how your body is feeling. Parts of you may feel tired and heavy, other parts may feel light and energized. Sometimes, if you start to relax, a bubbling laughter rises from your innards, like bubbles in a glass of lemonade. See if you can find the inner laugh and let it bubble up for you.

Anchoring

Imagine a time in your life when you felt very happy and confident. For some parents of bright kids it will be a recent memory, for others it may be a long time ago. Find that time, and notice where in your body you feel that feeling. For some it will be in your chest, for others your head, and for yet others it may be in your hands or arms. Now, with your writing hand, put the tip of your thumb and your index finger together and squeeze gently. Use this movement as a cue to remember this feeling of happiness and confidence. In the future, if times get tough, all you will need to do is to repeat that process of squeezing together the tips of your thumb and index finger of your writing hand to recall a time when things were better.

Mind clearing (clouds towards the horizon)

It takes time to think nothing. This is a restful exercise that teaches you how to clear your mind. It is estimated that people think an average of 13,000 thoughts every day. Unfortunately, most of those thoughts are the same ones they thought the day before.

Imagine yourself lying on an isolated beach. You are alone and safe. You can feel the warmth of the sunshine on your skin as the cool sea breeze washes over your body, cooling you and making you comfortable. The sound of the sea moving in and out against the sandy shore is like your breath moving gently in and out, in and out. Notice the sky with a few clouds. Imagine, as you sit restfully, that the sky begins to clear, and as it does your mind begins to empty of thoughts. Just as the last clouds reach the horizons, your mind attains clarity and focus.

Abdominal breathing

Sit comfortably with your spine straight. Breathe out completely, then breathe in very slowly and effortlessly through your nose, and at the same time push out your abdomen as though it were a balloon expanding.

Move your chest as little as possible. After your abdomen is stretched, expand your chest with air (this fills the middle part of your lungs), then allow your abdomen to pull in slightly and your shoulders and collarbones to rise (this fills the upper lungs).

Hold your breath for about five seconds, then slowly exhale through your nose.

Your own personal oasis
Throughout the ages, the oasis—a small patch of greenery in the middle of a desert—has held a special place in the imagination of travelers, who would dream of its cool waters, swaying palms, and beautiful birds in song. Take a moment to imagine your own personal oasis. Notice whether it has trees, and what type. Have you noticed if there is a well or a pool in the center? What other features can you imagine? Colors, shapes, sounds, scents ...

"So-hum"
"So-hum" is a yoga method for focusing the mind. It is useful at times of stress and upset. Sit in a chair with your backside to the back of the chair so you are sitting fairly upright. Place your hands in your lap. Either close your eyes or focus them on one of your hands. Breathe easily in and out through your nose. As you breathe in, say silently to yourself, "So," and as you breathe out, say slowly to yourself, "Hum." Try to extend the amount of time the "hum" takes. Some bright kids like to breathe out slowly while thinking to themselves, "One thousand, two thousand, three thousand ..."

Color kaleidoscope
Imagine that the way you are feeling now is a color. Close your eyes and select a color. Notice:

- what shape it is,
- what texture it has,
- if it is hot or cold,
- if it is sharp or soft, and
- if it is close or far away.

Now reduce the color to a softer shade. Repeat the procedure of noticing, then again soften its shade, and so on.

Creating happiness

The search for ways to motivate the "Click and Go" generation has led me to consider what creates happiness. For those interested in pursuing this research further, there is a world database of happiness available on the Internet (www.eur.nl/fsw/research/happiness/).

For the "Click and Go's"—with their short attention spans, their focus on immediate outcomes, and reliance on the external—the search for happiness could be a major motivator. But given that the world is a fairly unreliable provider of happiness, the "Click and Go's" reliance on external sources of satisfaction may be problematic.

> *"There are two kinds of lives: the horrible and the merely miserable."*
>
> Woody Allen

Generally, research indicates that despite having a level of material wealth that would boggle the eyes of even the wealthiest Indian maharaja of the past, we are, if anything, slightly less happy than we were 50 years ago. While a certain level of financial security is associated with happiness—and there is a tendency for wealthy countries to have more satisfied people—money doesn't have a lot to do with it. Thanks to our ability to adapt to ever-greater fame and fortune, yesterday's luxuries all too soon become today's necessities and tomorrow's garage sale items.

Aristotle concluded that, more than anything else, people seek happiness. Yet, it is elusive. In his book *Flow*, Mihaly Csikzentmihalyi—Professor of Psychology at the University of Chicago—points out that frustration is deeply woven into the fabric of life—whenever some of our needs are met, we immediately start wishing for more. The paradox is that with rising expectations, true quality of life is unattainable. Happiness is difficult to achieve partly because the universe was not designed with the comfort of human beings in mind. The world does not provide happiness. Happiness is created by people.

> *"Happiness is an agreeable sensation arising from contemplating the misery of others."*
> Ambrose Bierce

Contrary to what we may believe, happiness is not mostly associated with passive, relaxing times. We have an idea that whiling away the hours beside a pool at a tropical resort, a drink in hand and an object of desire nearby should be our happiest moment. While I am personally prepared to sacrifice myself to undertake further research in this area, it does appear that our happiest times aren't when we are passively relaxing but when we are being unselfconsciously absorbed in a mindful challenge—that is, an activity that immerses us in the experience so deeply that we forget to some extent about who we are and what our daily concerns are. After such experiences, we look up and think, "Where did the time go?" People often describe this state of being immersed in an experience as "flow."

These activities are ones where we have the skills to meet the challenge, and where the relationship between the challenges and the skills is balanced. If the challenge is too great, we experience anxiety. If the challenge is too easy, and we don't need to draw on our skills, we become bored. People report a range of activities that they engage in to develop a sense of flow: sports, games, socializing, drawing, art, music, reading, gardening, fishing, walking, playing with children or pets, even work.

The path to happiness

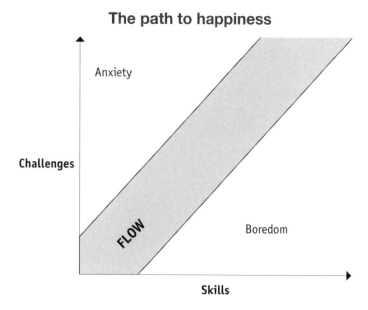

The distinctive feature of all these activities is that typically they involve people setting their own goals and providing their own rewards. It is by engaging in these activities that they free themselves from needing to wait for the outside world to provide challenges and rewards.

The knack of finding activities that produce this sense of flow in life is not something that children are often taught in their schools or homes. The pressure upon schools and time-poor parents to provide immediate gratification and entertainment for their children creates a maelstrom of activity that too often robs the young people of the opportunity of getting into flow.

> *"Happiness is an imaginary condition, formerly attributed by the living to the dead, now usually attributed by adults to children, and by children to adults."*
>
> Thomas Szasz

Our young people often experience a rush of stimulation, which may not cause anxiety but certainly increases arousal. Then, when the source of the stimulation is switched off, they wander around the house complaining, "I'm bored. There's nothing to do." Eventually they become passively dependent on the world to amuse and entertain them, and they believe they should always be happy. Invariably the world lets them down, because it is not a very reliable or fair provider of challenges and rewards, so they lose motivation. Even worse than losing motivation, it's all the world's (and that includes their parents') fault!

This can lead to a type of wistful envy: "If only we lived in a different area/closer to/further away from school"; "If only my parents were cool/had a better car/nicer house"; "If only I had a better group of friends." In time, this leads to a reliance on materialism and prevents young people from taking responsibility for creating a fulfilling life for themselves.

Helping bright kids create fulfilling lives

Helping young people find, engage in, and persist with activities that give them a sense of flow and happiness is crucial if they are to lead fulfilling lives. This requires slowing down at least some part of life so that young people can gradually engage in an activity over time, so they improve their performance and increase their pleasure. They need to persist with the activity, even though at times the challenges will seem too great. They must continue to challenge themselves when the performance seems to become too easy and, on the surface, boring.

These activities vary from person to person. For some it will be basketball or football, music or art, roller hockey or diving, writing or painting; for others it might be chess or skateboarding. You can't choose the activities that will give your child a sense of flow, but you can expose them to a range of activities and keep a keen eye out for those that absorb them. As a starting guide, a series of activities is listed on the following pages.

While happiness is not the sole key to motivation, it's not a bad starting place. To add to this we need to integrate what we have discussed here about fulfilment, motivation, and happiness.

Some sources of flow for young people

1. Taking a bath
2. Collecting things (e.g., shells)
3. Going on a vacation
4. Watching a favorite TV show
5. Going to the zoo
6. Playing/listening to music
7. Painting
8. Playing with a toy
9. Going to a party
10. Swimming
11. Laughing
12. Learning a joke
13. Practicing a magic trick
14. Drawing
15. Playing cards
16. Eating a favorite food
17. Sleeping over at a friend's place
18. Having a friend sleep over
19. Riding a bike
20. Playing a computer game
21. Doing a hobby
22. Growing plants or vegetables
23. Looking after/patting a pet
24. Going camping
25. Reading a comic book
26. Flying a kite
27. Milking a cow
28. Skateboarding
29. Canoeing
30. Playing with friends
31. Thinking about your birthday
32. Riding a scooter
33. Talking to your family
34. Roller blading
35. Learning to juggle
36. Going to Scouts
37. Sewing or knitting
38. Singing
39. Playing tennis
40. Gardening
41. Horse riding
42. Having your hair combed
43. Watching fireworks or a bonfire
44. Acting
45. Being in a choir
46. Skiing
47. Fishing
48. Making a present for someone
49. Taking photographs

50. Being alone
51. Eating chocolate
52. Running barefoot in a park
53. Visiting a playground
54. Playing volleyball
55. Watching or playing football
56. Shopping
57. Going to a museum
58. Remembering good times
59. Opening presents
60. Visiting an aquarium
61. Staying on a farm
62. Talking on the phone
63. Writing a letter
64. Flying in a plane
65. Playing softball
66. Writing a story
67. Doing jigsaw puzzles
68. Going bowling
69. Playing a musical instrument
70. Climbing a tree
71. Surfing a wave
72. Bouncing on a trampoline
73. Cooking
74. Dancing
75. Eating ice cream
76. Having lunch with a friend
77. Going on a picnic
78. Going to a movie
79. Passing a test at school
80. Making a new friend
81. Receiving a letter or a package
82. Having time to do nothing
83. Going out to dinner

Staying focused

> *"The main thing is to keep the main thing the main thing."*
> Stephen Covey

It is important to know that life is not fair. For that matter, school is not fair, either. The world doesn't generally reward you for being equally good at everything. In fact it usually only rewards you for two or three things you do well. One of the

tricks of success in life is to find your strengths and make much of them, and to not worry too much about areas where you are less capable. Here are some general guidelines to help you steer your bright kid towards developing a more fulfilling life:

- Help your bright kid become aware of her strengths and learn how to play to those. Be aware that your child's strengths may not always be valued by her school. For example, a Negotiator's verbal repartee and jokester behavior may not be highly regarded in third grade.

- Help her to promote a reputation that highlights her unique or exceptional attributes.

- Assist her to develop skills that increase her irreplaceability (i.e., a unique set of assets, knowledge, talents, and strengths that make her irreplaceable).

- Help your bright kid to seek out groups that most strongly value what she has to offer—where her assets will be cherished.

- Help your bright kid to avoid social groups where her unique attributes are not valued.

It is important to have high expectations of your child's ability to create a fulfilling life for herself, and to also expect her to have high expectations.

The world is going to be a very different place over the next few decades, and young people are going to need to be adaptable. If, as it is estimated, 70 percent of the jobs that will exist in the year 2020 don't exist yet, we cannot teach our children the knowledge they will need. What we can teach them, however, is to be excited and adept learners, and to maintain high expectations of themselves.

Forming true relationships

Probably nothing is more influential in career success and life happiness than the ability to get along with other people. Any parent who has ever tried to get children to share a cake will know this is not always the easiest lesson to learn.

"Reciprocators" are often happier people. The ability to work with others and to be considerate of their needs—that is, to reciprocate positive feelings—is an important predictor of life success as well as a source of resilience. Similarly, connectedness and a sense of belonging are the strongest antidotes we have to suicide, violence, and ongoing, problematic substance abuse.

It is our relationships with other people that give our lives meaning. An old Zulu saying puts this well: "People are people because of other people."

Teaching children to collaborate and to be sensitive to the needs of others requires them to develop an understanding of right and wrong. This requires parents to be assertively in charge of their families and to teach and keep teaching the one message that probably all the world's religions agree on: treat others as you would wish to be treated yourself.

Teach bright kids to control their competitiveness and to promote cooperation with other people.

It is also useful to help bright kids distinguish between true and fair-weather friends. Fair-weather friends are people who are there for you when times are good but disappear when times are tough. There is nothing wrong or bad about fair-weather friends, but we become upset—and bright kids become especially upset—when we confuse one with the other. When someone they thought was a true friend turns out to be a fair-weather friend, bright kids can be tempted to use the full force of their personality against that person. Learning that fair-weather friends are not bad people is a very important lesson for bright kids. It means that their friendships can endure and survive the ups and downs of life.

As well as true and fair-weather friends, there is also another category of friends that some bright kids attract: foul-weather friends. Foul-weather friends are people who show a lot of interest in you in times of trouble and need, but as soon as you cheer up or are out of difficulty, they don't want to know you. Help your bright kid understand that there are different types of friends. Share stories of your own experiences. Help him to be aware that not every friendship lasts a lifetime.

Bright kids can sometimes overestimate how many friends other people have, and can then conclude that they themselves are unpopular. In my clinical practice, I often ask children how many really close friends they have; the average is about two.

Takeaways

- Work out if your child is a "hot head" or a "cold heart."
- Be prepared to deal with a meltdown, and teach yourself and your bright kid how to calm down.
- Real happiness is created when we do things that absorb us so we enter a state of "flow."
- Bright kids have strengths that are often useful in adult life but are not valued during childhood.
- Demonstrate good friendship skills—knowing how to get along with others is an essential life skill.
- Bright kids need to be able to recognize their own strengths and talents.
- Help bright kids to differentiate between true, fair-weather, and foul-weather friends.

Part Five

TRICKY ISSUES

Life is rarely a smooth and even journey for anyone. Most families divide into two debating teams: one team wants things to change, the other team wants things to stay the same. The first team says things like, "I want to go out more," "I want more allowance," or "I don't want to be seen in public with you." The other team says things like, "You're not old enough" or "It's a school night, so you can't go out." For most families, parenting becomes a 28-year-long debating competition.

With bright kids, the debating competition has some added spices and flavors.

Even after using the change strategies in this book, there will be ups, downs, and setbacks. Don't despair. Part Five gives you some ideas for coping with the occasional setback, and also helps you steer your bright kid away from some of the major problems that could confront him or her.

23

When things get stuck

Here are some general principles that are useful if you find you are experiencing the same problems over and over again.

1. Step back from the problem and admit failure

Take a break from the problem! This allows you some space to look at what you are doing that may be contributing to the continuation of the problem. If you feel you are stuck, it may be worth considering what would happen if you did the reverse of what you are doing now. This may not always be possible, but it is worth accepting that doing more of what you are currently doing won't work either.

2. The problem is the problem

Rather than trying to blame yourself or your child, avoid spending much time on self-recrimination and blame. The problem is the problem, whether it be aggression, lack of motivation, drugs, alcohol, or school failure. The people involved are not.

There's not a lot of point in trying to work out why a problem exists; it's more important to work out how to get rid of it. Even if you work out exactly why you have a problem, you end up with an explanation but you still have the problem. Instead, use that energy to create a difference.

3. Notice what is happening when the problem isn't

Sometimes we become so burdened by the power of a problem, we don't notice what's going on when the problem isn't there. Keeping a diary each day can be helpful; notice what is going on either when the problem stops or when it is not around at all. If you can find out what's going on when there is no problem and make more of that happen, there will be less time for the problem to occur.

For example, you may like to ask yourself:

- What happens when she does her homework?
- How do these arguments we've been having end?
- What is happening differently when we don't argue?
- Who doesn't she fight with? How come?
- What happens when she does become motivated?

4. Behavior is linked to responses

Bright kids often behave to an audience—their parents. Try by all means to alter the behavior, but if that doesn't succeed try to change your response. As mentioned in Point 1, ask yourself what would happen if you did the reverse of what you normally do when the problem happens. Sometimes this won't be appropriate, but even so, it will probably start you thinking more productively about ways to change your response.

5. Aim small

Think about the smallest possible change that you could make to the problem. Don't try to solve the problem in one step. Try to change one little bit of it.

Most times, when people get stuck, it's because they are trying to shift a whole problem or pattern at one time. Most problems shift and free up if we make slight changes to day-to-day activities. More often than not, simple things will do. It may be useful to ask yourself, "What is the smallest change I could make that would have a positive effect on the problem right now?"

6. Pay attention to the child, not the behavior

It is easy to forget about your relationship with your child in the middle of a problem that keeps repeating. Generally it is not the child that is the problem. It is the behavior that is the problem. Whether the behavior is anger, fear, jealousy, or rage, everyone is pushed around by it, including the child or teenager.

One 17-year-old commented despairingly to me that his parents gave him all the responsibility and freedom of a 12-year-old, all the expectations of a 20-year-old, and forgot entirely that he had a 17-year-old's job to do. The message was clear: don't allow problem behavior to make your child invisible to you.

7. Stop being as predictable as a washing-machine cycle

For many bright kids, parents are about that predictable. They know what you are going to do before you have even thought of doing it. When things get stuck, look for ways to do things differently. As a wise old saying goes, craziness is doing the same thing over and over and expecting different results.

8. Get some help (call in the cavalry)

Some problems are too large, too concerning, or too serious to be handled alone, and it's important to know when things are out of control and you need outside help. The advice of other parents is invaluable, and while it takes a step of courage to ask someone else for ideas, you'll be surprised how flattered they will feel to be asked.

Professional assistance may be needed, however, when there is a risk to the long-term welfare of the family—such as in situations of physical violence, depression, self-harm, or suicidal tendencies.

Takeaways

Every family gets stuck from time to time. To get unstuck:

- Step back.
- Remember that the problem is the problem.
- Notice what's happening when the problem isn't.
- Know that behavior occurs in front of an audience.
- Aim small.
- Pay attention to the bright kids rather than their behavior.
- Change what you do.
- If need be, call in the cavalry.

24

Violence and depression

Violence and depression are two of the big fears for parents of bright kids: these kids might attract aggression, and they are also quite vulnerable to becoming depressed—as are their parents!

Violence and abuse

No one should experience violence. Violence between family members damages everyone's heart and spirit, and if it can't be contained, this means that the people involved can't live together. While violence includes verbal abuse and cruelty as well as emotional abuse and neglect, physical aggression is terribly damaging for young people. A large proportion of the young people that I have seen who attempted suicide did so after years of family conflict but only went on to attempt suicide after the conflict became physically violent.

Domestic violence—even when it doesn't directly involve the children—still breaks their spirits, and is a clear call for some form of professional help.

Sexual abuse within a family is an incredibly traumatic and confusing event that can literally drive people mad. If this is happening, get help. How to assist young people who have experienced sexual abuse is worth a whole book on its own. However, for families facing this issue, it's almost impossible to recover without the help of a skilled guide or counselor.

Depression

With bright kids exhibiting high levels of depression, referral to a mental health worker is also important. The teen years are notable for increases in self-deprecation, boredom, and depression.

Don't wait to act on this. The longer bright kids stay in one emotional state, the more familiar it becomes to them. Allowing an irritated bright kid to stay angry doesn't fix things. Leaving a sullen bright kid to experience sadness and despair for a while won't help. Bright kids rarely just grow out of problems.

Basically, the picture is that more young people today than ever before experience depression, and they begin feeling depressed at younger and younger ages. Middle adolescence (15–17 years) is a peak time for developing depression, and young women are at least twice as likely as young men to develop it. Some bright kids can get depressed at quite young ages.

The nasty news is that once you've experienced depression, you are more likely to experience it again and are more likely to have other problems such as substance abuse.

There are quite a few warning signs that may indicate suicide risk. Probably the most important is that the bright kid seems to be coping differently, compared with their usual way of living. Some people, after a period of unhappiness and depression, resolve to die, and then inexplicably anesthetize themselves to the decision. As a result, they cheer up. These people need to be asked firmly about a suicide plan, as they can repress it to the extent that they lose awareness of it. It is only by jolting them back through direct questioning that they can discuss it.

Any behavior that could be a rehearsal of a suicide should also cause concern. Some families report that their children changed their routines in strange ways such as taking to sleeping in their clothes, keeping the windows open at night in winter, sleeping in odd places, visiting cemeteries, going to school erratically, or not washing regularly in the weeks prior to making a suicide attempt. Others noted that they seemed less happy, more switched-off, bleaker than usual, or generous in giving away personal items.

If there is an inexplicable change in a bright kid's functioning and if you feel more worried than usual about him, ask. It is always better to overreact than underreact. If your bright kid says he feels life is not worth living, insist he sees someone with you to sort it out. If he refuses, drag him along. If he still refuses, consult a mental health professional you trust.

The most consistent warning sign of suicide that we have is hopelessness and depression. Bright kids don't always get depressed in the same way adults do. Adults talk about being sad, mope around, drink more cheap wine, eat more chocolate, and generally convey their misery. Bright kids may talk of being bored or "pissed off" rather than feeling sad; they may become more irritable and harder to live with; their concentration may suffer; they may use more drugs, they may become either almost totally inactive or restless and pacing; and they may eat less. Others will write bleak poetry, speak of suicide and death, and listen to morbid music.

Given that most bright kids who become depressed have not been the cheeriest to begin with, working out if they are feeling more hopeless than usual can be very difficult. When hopelessness invades all areas of their life and they lose their ability to shake off self-absorption or to consider others' feelings, it's time to feel anxious about their wellbeing.

Self-care is another warning sign I find useful. Increased risk-taking behavior such as substance abuse, sexual behavior, deliberate self-harm, and dangerous driving should always be taken as possible signs of depression and despair.

Takeaways

- Take violence and depression seriously. It is better to overreact and get some help than to underreact.
- If bright kids don't want to see a mental health professional, say to them, "I need you to come and see someone with me at least once so I can know whether I should worry or not."

25

From lying to honesty

Some bright kids will do whatever it takes, including lie, to get the outcome they want. They need to learn there is more to be gained from being honest than from lying.

Fibs, boasts, and "whoppers"

By three years of age, some children lie. By at least four years of age, they know that it is wrong to mislead someone but they don't really understand why it is wrong. Later in this chapter is a summary of children's understanding of truthfulness at different ages.

Lies come in different shapes and sizes. There is the bare-faced lie intended to deceive and mislead, there's sneaky behavior and there's non-committal communication. Here's an example of the latter:

> *"How was the party?"*
> *"Okay."*
> *"Who was there?"*
> *"Everyone."*
> *"What did you do?"*
> *"Not much."*

Most of us lie from time to time—let's not forget Santa Claus, the Tooth Fairy, and the Easter Bunny! If lying becomes a major habit, it erodes trust and goodwill in a family. Parents often report feeling guarded, used, and abused when their bright kid lies frequently. Developing a habit of lying is associated with stealing, having negative friends, vandalism, and school truancy.

The pathway to honesty

Bright kids who habitually lie have often been getting away with it for some time, and can even begin to believe their own lies. So how can we get them back to honesty?

The first thing to do is to build a family in which people are expected to do what they say they will do. You will need to model this to your children.

The second thing is to have a rule of no excuses. Excuses are the breeding ground of lies. Either you are going to do something or you are not—there are no excuses.

Children's understanding ...

Age	Understanding of what is right	Reason to be good
4	Getting my own way—fairness is my way.	Get rewards and avoid punishment.
5–6	Doing what you're told (by grown-ups).	Not get into trouble—"How would I feel if someone lied to me?"
6–8	Doing unto others exactly what they do to you.	"What's in it for me?" Tit-for-tat mentality.
8–12	Living up to others' expectations, pleasing others.	So others think well of me and so I think well of myself. Adults are not always right. Self-image as a good person —will lie to avoid displeasure.
12–14	Having a clear understanding of right and wrong, but will lie for popularity reasons and to mislead. May lie by omission.	Loyalty to friends. Self-image as a good person.
15–16	Being intellectually clear about right and wrong but still not always thinking through consequences.	Truthfulness can be seen as a commodity that some people deserve and others do not.
17–	Fulfilling obligations to friends, family, and society.	Honesty is a positive attribute in a good person.

Third, parents need to be the judges of truth. If you are doubtful about something you are being told by your bright kid, cross your arms, look at them seriously, and say, "I'm not sure about that. Convince me."

Fourth, responding angrily to lies is rarely useful. It is better to say something like, "That is very creative [or imaginative]—now tell me something I can believe." Bright kids do best when they believe their parents have eyes in the back of their head, and so can't be fooled.

Fifth, if a lie is found out, the child must make up for it in some way that restores trust.

The understanding bright kids have of honesty changes as they grow up (see the table below). It may give you some insight into how to help.

... of truthfulness

Main parenting strategy
Don't expect to make great inroads into their understanding about lying. If they state an inaccurate version of events, calmly remind them what actually happened.
Build a family culture of truthfulness by not allowing misleading information or sneaky behavior to result in positive outcomes for your child.
Start to emphasize compassion by asking what would it be like to be in that person's position. Explain what would happen if everyone lied.
As friendship patterns can shift in this age range, teach them that honesty is a good friendship skill. If conflict with friends occurs, discourage putting others down or spreading rumors.
Critical time for building truthfulness. Give opportunities to be trusted but be vigilant. For example, if your child wants to stay over at Harry's, you might say, "Okay, but is there anything I should know before I call his parents?"
Assist them to predict outcomes by asking them "What do you think would happen if ...?"-type questions.
Community service opportunities (though not everyone gets to this stage).

Lying and the different types of bright kids

Manipulators
Some lie to impress others and to look good. Ensure they know their personal best effort is good enough. Praise honesty.

Negotiators
With Negotiators, make sure you have a clear policy of fixing the lie rather than emphasizing the fault.

Competitors
Competitors' lies can often be boastful, and these bright kids can feel they have to live up to their own lies. Discourage them from talking too freely about their great "victories."

Debaters
Unless there is *clear* evidence of a lie, do not implement consequences. Talk to them about your observations, not your opinions.

Dare Devils
Lies can have major consequences for Dare Devils. If lying becomes a pattern, it can lead to very risky behavior in unsupervised circumstances.

Passive Resisters
For Passive Resisters, lying can be a way of evading participation and responsibility. They may lie about feeling unwell to avoid social activities and family outings. Supervise them closely, and if illness becomes a persistent excuse, take them to a doctor.

Takeaways

- Lying is a common issue with bright kids.
- The reasons why kids lie change as they grow up, and the strategies parents need to use to build trust and honesty also have to change.

26

Peer-group pressure

The friends your bright kid chooses to mix with may not always be the ideal comrades you were hoping for. The solution is for your child to have diverse friendship groups.

The secret world

Parenting is different and scarier these days because there is a world of peer pressure that occurs outside the inkling of adults. Cell phones, email, messaging, and texting are almost impossible to keep track of.

Many bright kids have two worlds: the world of peers where they need to be cool, compact, and calculating; and the world of family, where they can still be young and make mistakes. Parents shouldn't expect bright kids to behave with their peers in the same way they behave with them.

The rule of the 3 F's

The absolute first thing to do is to get to know their peers. Knowing them and, if you can, their parents places you in a much more powerful position. Find them, feed them, and (be)friend them.

Don't forget that peer-group pressure can be positive as well as negative. Having a strong positive link with a few key players in your child's life increases the chances that the pressure will be positive.

Peer pressures parents worry about

"You're fat, go on a diet."
"You're ugly."
"It's cool to goof around at school."
"Stop being such a nerd."
"Try this drug, it's cool."
"How about we borrow this car and go for a midnight drive?"

It's enough to keep any parent awake at night. The world of friendship for many children is, in reality, a world of ruthless, vindictive, nasty competitiveness. People will say horrible things to your child, especially if he is a bright kid.

THE INJURY ALWAYS JUSTIFIES THE WIN!!!

Bright kids who are the feistiest can also be the most susceptible to the pressures and influences of others. Teach your child to differentiate opinion from reality. Talk about opinions you have that most people probably don't share. Ask your child to describe an opinion he has, and discuss whether it is reality. For example:

"What is your favorite color?
"Do you think everyone in the whole world has that color as their favorite?
(Hopefully he'll say "No," but if he says "Yes," say, "Okay, let's do a survey, and ask ten people.")

"So if you were to say that [your favorite color] was the best color, what would happen? Most likely, some people would agree and others would disagree. Your favorite color is just your opinion, and their favorite color is just their opinion. Most opinions are like that."

Another exercise I often do with kids who are concerned about what people think of them is to get a series of photos of people from magazines and ask them to score those people out of 10 for beauty, and then ask them to compare that with how other people might rate them. Trying to get them to see that beauty is just an opinion is not always easy, but the aim is to at least get them to understand that not everything other people say is true.

Say to your bright kid, "Don't believe everything that other people say about you. If you are really worried, check it out by asking others."

Peer pressure at different ages

Belonging is the driving force behind peer pressure, and it can be either healthy or distorted (see the tables in Chapter 15 for more on this).

During the preschool years, children engage in independent play, so there is generally little peer pressure. The tasks of sharing toys and attention are the two main issues at this stage.

During primary school, there are often clusters of friendships, with boys and girls usually in different groups. There will be a strong awareness of who gets invited to parties and for sleepovers.

The early high-school years see friendship clusters—girls' groups are tighter, more exclusive, and more status-conscious than boys'. The degree of the child's physical development is important here.

A survey of school students about words they associate with popularity is revealing:

Age	Boys	Girls
17	Friendly Influential Cool	Friendly Confident Nice
16	Friends Leader Friendly	Friends Happy Outgoing
15	Me Friends Cool	Nice Friendly Friends
14	Friends Sex Drugs	Attractive Friends Boys
13	Cool Friends Attractive	Friends Attractive Cool
12	Cool Well-known Friends	Attractive Friends Fashionable
11	Friends Cool Kind	Pretty Friends Cool
10	Cool Funny Friends	Friends Pretty Cool
9	Cool Liked Clever	Cool Liked Clever
8	Cool Playful Great	Cool Friends Clever
7	Cool Liked Famous	Friendly Special Liked
6	Kind Nice Helpful	Kind Helpful Pretty

Apart from showing how powerful perceived prettiness is even at age six for girls, the table also indicates that popularity in the later teen years has more to do with social skills and confidence than appearance.

Diversify

Alongside knowing your child's peers as a way of countering negative peer pressure, is diluting that pressure. Ensuring that your bright kid has a range of friends not only contributes to her resilience, but also means she is less likely to be led astray by a few others. Strategies for diversifying the peer group include travel, youth groups, broadening your connection with your extended family, changing schools, and, in some cases, moving away from the area you live in.

Peer pressure and the different types of bright kids

Parents often speak about the sorts of negative peer pressure that affect their bright kid. Let's look at these.

Manipulators

Manipulators can be the source of negative peer pressure on others. Teach them to be direct in their dealings with others. Have a zero-tolerance approach to rumor-spreading, bullying, or talking behind others' backs.

Negotiators

Negotiators are often regarded as "cool" by others. Divide and conquer: *never* negotiate with them in front of their peers.

Competitors

The pressure that Competitors feel to be better than anyone else can lead to loneliness and vulnerability to taunts and bullying from others. Help them to differentiate between fair-weather and true friends.

Debaters

Peers can usually play Debaters like a fiddle. Debaters' natural courage can lead them into battle on behalf of the insincere.

Dare Devils

Oh, dear! A gaggle of Dare Devils hanging out together is a recipe for parental anxiety. Try to make sure your Dare Devil has a variety of friends, including some calmer types. When Dare Devils do mix with other Dare Devils, make sure it is in structured situations, such as organized sport.

Passive Resisters

One special friend can make all the difference to a Passive Resister. These bright kids may associate for a time with younger peers. Try to give them a mix of ages to socialize with, including your own friends.

Takeaways

Get to know your child's peers by using the rule of the "3 F's":
- Find them.
- Feed them.
- (Be)Friend them.

27
Perfectionism

Perfectionism is the biggest killer of motivation that I know of. Unless we tackle it head on, it will stop many bright kids in their tracks and make them avoid trying out new activities and adventures.

The quest for perfection

Does your bright kid pay more attention to his mistakes than to his correct answers? Does he have unrealistic expectations of his work? Is getting an A– rather than an A+ a major catastrophe? Does he get upset at anything in life that doesn't work perfectly? If so, welcome to the world of the perfectionist.

Like the pot of gold at the end of the rainbow, perfection is impossible. As Salvador Dalí once commented, "Have no fear of perfection—you'll never reach it." But despite the unattainability of it all, perfectionism has an invasive grip over the lives of many bright kids.

I WAS THE ONLY ONE IN CLASS WHO KNEW LANCE ARMSTRONG'S FAVORITE UNDERWEAR COLOR!

VICTORY OR SUPA QUIZ

A+

Perfectionism can be a cause of both stress and positive behavior. It drives some people to great achievements far beyond their wildest dreams. Mix it with a punishing attitude, however, and it can stifle imagination and crush the spirit. Also, what's great for achievement is not always great for relationships.

Don't get me wrong here: I like a certain amount of perfectionism in my dentists, airline pilots, taxi drivers, and surgeons. The issue here is the amount of it and the effect it has on your child.

The procrastinators' club

Procrastination is a problem affecting all perfectionists. Many bright kids can become paralyzed perfectionists—they are so scared of getting it wrong, they can't get it right. The response of some bright kids to perfectionism is to shy away from activities they believe they can't do well at. This can restrict their lives.

Parents can help perfectionist bright kids by:

- *increasing spontaneity in the family.* Taking the family on a picnic on the spur of the moment, or suddenly changing your mind and dragging the family to see a new movie, allows perfectionist bright kids to learn that the world is not a controllable place.

- *breaking down activities into subtasks.* For example, rather than focusing on the score in a tennis match, emphasize how well your child served. This also increases awareness of how a particular skill is performed, rather than obsessing over the outcome of the game. Too much emphasis on outcomes increases anxiety and reduces performance.

- *encouraging continuous improvement.* Set goals but focus on improvement. For instance, it took Einstein 20 attempts to properly formulate his Special Theory of Relativity. Another good example of improvement is John Naber, who, at the 1972 Olympics, watched Mark Spitz win seven gold medals in swimming, one of which was in the 100-meter backstroke— Naber's own event. Naber envisioned himself winning gold in Montreal in 1976, and worked out that he would need to improve his time by four seconds to achieve this. He had four years to achieve his dream. Naber worked out that he had to improve one second per year. Since he swam twice a day, he only needed to improve by 1/730th of a second per workout. In 1976 he won gold.

■ *focusing on their personal best.* Some bright kids will see their "best" in terms of results alone, but for many it may be best to focus on effort.

Perfectionism and the different types of bright kids

This is an area where bright kids vary markedly from one another. Some become anxious and fretful when suffering from perfectionism, others become listless and defeated. Some common patterns are outlined here.

Manipulators
Manipulators can be so successful in engineering outcomes that they can come to believe they can control the world. They need to learn the world is not a controllable place, and the best way for this to happen is for parents to act in unexpectedly spontaneous ways.

Negotiators
These bright kids are the most likely to avoid anything they don't feel they are competent at. As they are so aware of the audience, helping them to try things out the first time, away from the gaze of peers, is helpful.

Competitors
Introduce the "pizza theory of talents": just as many and varied slices make up a pizza, so all of us have different talents. Some might have one or two slices of talent, some might have more. Some might have only one slice of talent but it is strongly flavored. It's not about having more talents than anyone else, it's about what you do with the talents you have.

Debaters
The social-justice instincts of these economic rationalists means they would like a perfect world. Help them to see that their marks at school are not measures of their personal self-worth. Turn their complaints into effective action.

Dare Devils
Break tasks down into mini-tasks and time-trials for Dare Devils. Use their level of focus on and application to these mini-tasks as the measure of success.

Passive Resisters
Don't allow them to opt out. Passive Resisters can decide that the best way to preserve their dignity is not to attempt anything, really. Having strong family expectations that they will engage in some activities such as sports, music, and hobbies helps them to stay connected and to flourish.

Takeaways

- Perfectionism stops bright kids from trying out new things, and reduces resilience.
- Increase spontaneity in your family activities.

28

Sexuality

Bright kids belong to a generation of young people that has been bombarded with sexual images. At times it seems as if we are witnessing the disappearance of late childhood as it races into adolescence. We live in a society that often treats childhood as an ailment to be remedied as quickly as possible—and if you can medicate kids along the way, that's even better.

Parents of bright kids need to be vigilant to preserve the time of childhood. Bright kids are often interested in foregoing childhood interests, and instead want to rush into adolescence.

It does no one any favors to have bright kids grow up before their time. Parents need to keep bright kids strongly attached to the family through family-based activities, and need to be prepared to say "No" to the viewing of some movies or the playing of some computer games. The world will place enough pressure on your child to become a sex god or goddess before his or her time. For bright kids, early initiation into this world often leads to risk taking in many ways.

Alternative sexuality

The process of discovering their sexual orientation is difficult enough for every teenager, and it can be especially so for young people who suspect that they are gay, lesbian, or bisexual. The early discovery of these feelings often creates confusion in young people and their parents.

Part of this confusion is that people try to sort out whether these feelings represent a phase the young person is going through or whether they are part of an ongoing orientation. Some young gay people say that they knew of their orientation from their early teens or even before, whereas others struggle to understand their feelings of attraction and desire for most of their lives. Generally, trying to categorize young people into the "passing phase" or the "ongoing orientation category" is not particularly helpful.

Try to understand that young people may initially feel isolated and confused as well as unsure about their own feelings. This process may affect their self-esteem as they try to determine where they belong. Parents often deal with this by restating their love for their child and their trust that the child will eventually find what is right for her. It is not useful to say, "Don't worry dear, I'll love you anyway," as young people sometimes hear this as, "Despite this awful disappointment, I'll put up with you and put on a happy face." Instead, simply tell them that you love them and home is where they belong.

Some young people, as they explore their alternative sexuality, go though a process of checking out people's responses and being very sensitive to these responses. This is a roller-coaster time, with some great highs and some dreadful lows. For a time, their sexual orientation can become the biggest thing in their lives, which can create conflict in families.

One young man recollected that he'd been a pain to his family when he discovered his homosexuality: "It was like I was on a crusade. They would have their friends over and I'd start up a discussion about homosexuality just to watch them squirm. I guess I didn't want them to ignore or gloss over what was happening to me."

For most gay, lesbian, and bisexual young people, relationships eventually become more important than sexual orientation. Then they have just got to deal with the usual issues of finding the right person, falling in love, falling out of love, trying to find the next right person, and so on. Simple, isn't it?

For the parents of young people going through tough times, life can be incredibly stressful and distressing. Ensuring that you get the help that you need to maintain your own ability to cope and to lead the way is essential.

Takeaways

- The mixture of bright kids and sex can be intoxicating, frightening, and alarming for parents.
- It does no one any favors to have bright kids mature before their time.
- Discourage age-inappropriate sexualized clothing and mannerisms.

29

Survival skills for parents

Michelangelo was reportedly once asked what he did for a living. He didn't answer that he was an artist; instead, he described his work as a sculptor as a process of removing the excess marble concealing the beauty of the figure within. His job, he was reported to have said, was a process of uncovering rather than creating. Parenting bright kids is just like this.

Bright kids are the people who can change the world. They are the people with all the spirit, energy, and get-up-and-go to make a difference. They are vigorous survivors. For them to broaden out to become the people they really can be, they need parents who not only survive but thrive.

Parents of bright kids need good ears, a good heart, and a good spirit.

"Good ears"

By "good ears," I mean being able to quiet your own inner conversation and listen to your child, to hear the nuances of their stories, the values they express, and the hopes, dreams, and despair contained within them. This is an ongoing challenge because most people have two ways of being with others: talking and waiting to talk.

"Clean your ears" and rid yourself of everyday prejudices, assumptions, and short-hand ways of summarizing what people are saying. It is always easier to presume rather than to listen, but bright kids are not like everyone else: they have talents, skills, and vulnerabilities that are a unique and powerful mix.

Parents of bright kids often need to listen "behind the words." Bright kids, in the heat of battle, can say the most hurtful, heart-shattering things. Being able to listen behind the words to the fearfulness and anxiety allows parents to remain calm in stormy times and to preserve goodwill in their family.

A good heart

"A good heart" refers to being able to view people compassion-ately, to see the positives in bright kids and their actions—that is, to be able to see beyond the behavior to the underlying values and to what the behavior is *really* trying to achieve.

The great drive of many bright kids can elicit in some adults a desire to control them. But bearing in mind these kids' great potential, and being prepared to reveal the beauty of the figure within, allows parents to avoid engaging in pointless battles.

Parents of bright kids receive a lot of advice. Much of it is unhelpful, of the "spare the rod and spoil the child" variety. Having a good heart also refers to being compassionate to yourself. No one has all the answers to parenting bright kids, but no one knows your bright kid better than you do. We all make mistakes from time to time and lose our cool or our perspec-tive. At the end of the day, what matters is not that you were a perfect parent but that you were prepared to do what you could, by remaining a fierce friend to your bright kid, owning up when you made errors, doing what you said you would do, and maintaining as positive a relationship as you could.

I've heard that Mozart once wrote a musical composition that was so harmonically perfect, so technically balanced that it was, well, a bit soulless and dull. He then rewrote the piece, adding some dissonant passages and some notes that continued on for longer than was usually expected in pieces of this type to create some tension and drama. In some ways, people are like this: it is our imperfections that make us interesting.

A good spirit

"A good spirit" requires taking time out for self-nourishing. Parenting is the hardest and the best job going around, and parenting bright kids is like running an endurance race on a dark night in a blizzard. Taking the time out to sleep well, to acquaint yourself with what is happening in the world outside your home, and, above all, to laugh, not only helps you maintain perspective, it makes you a better parent.

Clarissa Pinkola Estés, who wrote *Women Who Run With the Wolves*, has a wonderful concept called the "hand-crafted life." Each person is a little like a potter, shaping, honing, and refining the overall pattern of their lives. It is easy, and sometimes inevitable, to have your life shaped by other people or outside forces; however, you are in charge of preserving your own uniqueness.

Bright kids often have an immense desire to fit in, even if it costs them their own individuality. Having a parent who can nourish difference, who teaches the art of being socially successful while celebrating originality, helps bright kids to not lose sight of their great strengths and talents. Having a parent who preserves and cherishes his or her own uniqueness shows bright kids that it is all right to be themselves.

Bright kids don't need to be "fixed" because they aren't broken. They do, however, need to be shown ways to play to their own strengths and to learn a range of ways to interact with the world. They need to be shown how to flourish and thrive, and parents are the best people to do this.

In order to "hand-craft" your own life, you have to be a bit of a subversive, a counter-revolutionary. In a world where people rush faster and faster, work longer and longer, and laugh less and less, it is important to remember that it is our connections to other people—especially our families—that give meaning to our lives.

It is also worth reminding ourselves of the four essential questions asked in many forms of traditional healing:

- When did you stop singing?
- When did you stop dancing?

- When did you stop listening to and telling stories?
- When did you become disenchanted with the sacred place of silence?

Takeaways

Maintain yourself and your sanity by keeping:

- good ears,
- a good heart,
- a good spirit, and
- a healthy sense of fun.

Part Six

A SUPPLEMENT FOR THE TEACHERS OF BRIGHT KIDS

In every school there are two types of students:

1. your nice, agreeable, friendly, lovable students, and
2. the bright ones who have a mind of their own. They can be fiery and feisty, argumentative, and downright sneaky.

Bright kids are not bad kids; they simply tried out a particular behavior that worked for them, so they keep on using it.

There is a paradox that faces most teachers: those young people who leave school to go on and do remarkable things are not always the easiest to teach. Sadly, history does not record the thoughts of the teachers of Joan of Arc, Napoleon Bonaparte, Charles de Gaulle, or Abraham Lincoln as they left school. But that, rather than having much of a tear in their eye, the response might have been more like, "Phew, I'm glad *that's* over. Now they can change the world while I can have a bit of rest."

Bright kids can vary from lovable rogues to absolute pains in the rear end. They certainly have their strengths, but tackle them in the incorrect way and they can make your life a misery.

This supplement is to try to assist you to identify some of the common behaviors of bright kids and to devise strategies for helping them to flourish into the people they truly could become—while preserving your sanity in the process.

A sanity kit for the teachers of Manipulators

Motto: "Whatever it takes!"

Manipulators:

- can wrap teachers around their little finger, eat them for breakfast, hoodwink them, and charm the socks off them,
- can bully other children,
- are very, very good at playing cute to adults,
- are determined and somewhat single-minded, and
- are extremely ambitious and goal-focused.

One great example is Angelica from *Rugrats* (see Chapter 2 for more examples).

Common strengths	Common vulnerabilities
- Bright. - Focused. - Clever. - Ambitious. - Goal-oriented. - Fantastic leadership potential.	- When they fall out with friends, they usually do so in a big way. They not only need to be the center of attention, they have to be the best. Their self-esteem is not based on anything positive. - They work from the idea that the end justifies the means. - If winning (or impressing adults) requires that they lie, cheat, or denigrate others, they will do it. - Their moral reasoning can be based on expediency.

Helping Manipulators to change

Congratulations, you have a bright, focused, ambitious, goal-directed child with fantastic leadership potential in your class.

Being the teacher of a Manipulator takes thinking through. The first thing is that it can take a while before you identify all of the Manipulators in your class. Some of them are camouflaged by niceness. Some of them are the high-flying students of your school. Look for the kids who always want to be top dog, at almost any cost. Look for the kids who other children are careful not to upset. Sometimes very popular children can be Manipulators.

...AND I'D LIKE TO THANK MY PARENTS FOR THEIR SUPPORT!

Make sure you contact the parents of these kids early in the year, and get them on your side. If an incident does occur, you are much more likely to be successful if your relationship with the parent(s) is positive.

Remember, many of these kids can lie without guilt, and have had years of practice at making themselves look good to adults. Many parents of Manipulators are in denial; some will argue for their children against all reason. If this is the case, don't spend hours trying to convince the unpersuadable. Instead, direct your energies towards helping the child flourish at school.

Manipulators have heaps of skills to develop, and can grow up to be wonderful contributors to society. They do, however, need to learn to give up their sneaky ways. Manipulators change when they finally encounter an adult who:

- has got their number,
- can call them out, and
- has eyes in the back of his or her head.

With Manipulators, I recommend asking one school staff member to take on that student as a "personal change" project. The idea is that the staff member will make it their business to catch up regularly with the Manipulator—so much so that the child rarely has an inch to move. For example, the staff member on lunchtime playground duty might say to the Manipulator, "Come on, you're coming with me." The Manipulator might then plead and complain, "But I haven't done anything wrong." To which the staff member responds, "No, but you might. Come on."

What is always fascinating to watch in schools is the process Manipulators go through when we do this. At first they will whine and carry on, and say something like, "It's not fair, why do I have to stay with you? I want to play with my friends." After a while, however, they form a bond with that adult unlike any other connection they have ever had. This is because, for the first time, they have encountered an adult who has them really worked out. The comfort that the Manipulators feel may not always be expressed immediately as gratitude, but they are usually able to change and broaden as people.

In the classroom, use structured group work with alternating roles and leadership. Keep mixing the students into different groupings. Introduce a healthy relationship program, including bullying prevention, and redirect their leadership abilities in a positive manner. As Manipulators can be fantastic leaders, get them to take on different constructive roles; be prepared to temporarily take away the extra role if they begin to act negatively.

Manipulators can engage in covert nastiness against other children. After such an incident, have all the students involved write down their account of it. Keep these records on file.

Confront Manipulators at their own game and take a pro-active role, with much more adult supervision. Probably the worst situation in a school is when two Manipulators fight it out for supremacy of the social territory. This is anything but angelic! Separate them. Confront each one directly. Put them on notice and then engage the support of other staff to keep a close eye on them.

A sanity kit for the teachers of Negotiators

Motto: "There's always another audience!"

Negotiators:

- are as sharp as a tack,
- are wheeler-dealers who can run rings around you if you are not careful,
- always have another option—if you've got two options, they'll have three,
- are cunning, conning, and funny,
- control by resisting direction and requests,
- engage other people by being jokesters (and they are generally good at it), and
- don't know when to stop.

One great example is Bart Simpson (see Chapter 3 for more examples).

Common strengths	Common vulnerabilities
<ul><li>Extremely talented at twisting and turning words into humor, provocation, or distraction.</li><li>Fiercely independent.</li><li>Engaging.</li><li>Funny.</li><li>Sharp-witted.</li><li>Knowledgeable.</li><li>Lots of street smarts.</li></ul>	<ul><li>Use distraction to get out of any area in which they might fail.</li><li>Truth is a very shiftable commodity.</li><li>Don't want to show you they are compliant: a dismissive shrug of the shoulder or a wise-crack is often all the response you will get.</li><li>Love an audience for their jokes and actions.</li></ul>

Helping Negotiators to change

Over the years, teachers have come to me at their wits' end, saying something like, "I never want to teach that child ever again" or "Hang that child by his toenails from the rafters." This tells me they have a master Negotiator in their class.

We all run the risk of becoming our own worst enemy with the Negotiators of this world. The reason is, they *are* funny. Really funny. So we laugh along with them. By enjoying a joke with them, we are led into mistakenly believing we have some goodwill with that child. Then, out of the blue, that same child turns around and does something incredibly annoying and irritating. We can feel this as a personal betrayal.

In a friendship, feeling betrayed might be an appropriate response. In a classroom setting, you need to realize that it is not personal. All the Negotiators are doing is playing to a larger audience.

Negotiators can be engaging, sharp-witted, knowledgeable students with the comedic skills of Charlie Chaplin. Unfortunately, you also have someone who could drive you mad. There has been a long history of these type of kids in children's literature: Tom Sawyer, Huckleberry Finn, Dennis the Menace, and, of course, Bart Simpson. Don't be fooled by the fact that all these potential candidates for serious medication were boys— Negotiators can be girls as well.

Five strategies

The first thing you need to do when teaching Negotiators is to have a strategy for removing the audience. If you have no such strategy, you have no strategy *at all*. Possible methods include sending the child to an understanding colleague's classroom, to "Admin," or even the whole class leaving the room.

Second, decide on one or two key bottom lines that you can hold steadfastly with this student for a minimum of six weeks. Be clear about the behavior that you want to see more of, and don't try to achieve too much. Let me repeat that: *don't try to achieve too much.* Teachers typically overestimate the amount of change that can occur and underestimate the time it will take. As a rule of thumb, if you are changing one of the Negotiator's negative behaviors every six weeks, you are doing so well you deserve a medal of honor. Two behaviors every six weeks is the absolute maximum. Get the support of other teachers to help you with this.

Third, tell the student: "This is what I want you to do." Inform him that there will be consequences if he does not do this. Don't expect Negotiators to believe you. They have had years of outsmarting adults, so one clear message isn't going to faze them. They will be convinced only by actions, not words.

Fourth, there is no point arguing with Negotiators. All that happens is that they get an adrenaline rush and an entertained audience. When they are behaving in ways that are counter to your one or two bottom lines, approach them as quietly and calmly as possible. Whisper to them, "You are breaking our agreement. You can either stop that now or face the consequences—you have a choice." Withdraw for about a minute. If the misbehavior continues, implement your audience-removal strategy. The consequences for the misbehavior can be put into place later, at a time that is more convenient to you. One useful consequence is to require students to come into school early, to help you prepare for the day. They can be allocated tasks such as photocopying and cleaning. This also helps them to learn responsibility.

Fifth, during the six weeks, try to find other ways for Negotiators to gain peer approval by mixing them with students they don't normally associate with or by giving them positions of responsibility or even privilege.

An additional note: these kids eat substitute teachers for breakfast! Be kind to your substitute teachers by creating a file on your strategy, so if you are away they can at least have *some* chance of success.

A sanity kit for the teachers of Debaters

Motto: "Whoever has the last word, wins!"

Debaters:

- are determined,
- often dispute things and don't give in,
- are well suited to a career in the law courts, and
- have often learned at home to argue with brothers and sisters, and they bring this well-honed skill into your classroom.

One great example is the former British Prime Minister, Margaret Thatcher (see Chapter 4 for more examples).

Common strengths	Common vulnerabilities
- Strong sense of fairness and right and wrong. - Very verbal—can use language well. - Energetic to the point of being driven. - Analytical skills of an expert prosecutor.	- Can be indignant. - Will argue the point. - Is often not tuned in to their own emotions. - Is aware of resentment and a lack of fairness, but that disguises an insecurity about whether they are good enough and lovable enough.

Helping Debaters to change

"I put it to you that at 2:13 p.m. last Thursday, when your back was turned, Michael ate my piece of chocolate while Sally scribbled in my book and Emily smirked at me. A great travesty of justice has occurred!"

No, you are not in a courtroom, you are listening to a Debater complain to his or her teacher. You have in your class a student with the verve, energy, and analytical skills of an expert prosecutor, able to debate, cite examples, and refute defensive teachers in a single bound. Having a Debater in your class is like teaching a Human Rights Commissioner. "It's not fair" is a claim you may hear a lot.

Minor variations in procedures can escalate into major infringements of human liberty, fraternity and egalitarianism. You'll hear claims like:

"It's not fair, [choose any of the following:]
I didn't get four minutes on the computer."
I wasn't allowed out till I finished the work."
my piece of chocolate cake is not as big as ..."
I had to bring my own pencil. Why doesn't ... have to bring theirs?"
The list is endless, and is often accompanied by: "And I'll get my Mom [or Dad] up here to talk to you about this!"

You can end up in incredible knots with these kids as you try to justify the fairness of it all: "No, *it is* fair, because last week when you were away at the dentist, Mick missed out on two minutes on the computer, Sally had a smaller piece of chocolate cake, David finished his work early, and Briony brought her own pencil," you might reply.

It's enough to send you around the twist! Unless you want to become a rule-bound teacher who rigidly applies the same procedures to everyone, whether they need it or not, you'll have to find another way to handle complaints from the Debaters.

First, allow them to briefly articulate their point of view. Restate your decision and then, rather than going for justification, aim for empathy.

"You must be finding it difficult/be upset that this time you didn't get the biggest piece/more computer time." Try to be kind and understanding, but don't offer to shift your position.

Sometimes Debaters will want to continue the discussion. If so, say something like, "I'm really interested and would like to hear more about it another time. Come and chat with me at the end of the day."

If they do come to see you later, ask them to explain and then ask them to tell you what would make it fair. Don't promise to do what they suggest. Just listen, then say, "Thanks for your ideas."

With Debaters, it's important to recognize that you don't have to solve the issue right away. In fact it's often a good idea to be caring but not particularly useful in resolving their complaints.

If they do grind you to the point where you shift your position, be honest about it and say something like, "You're right, it would be fairer the way you suggested." Don't shift your position too much, though. If you do, you teach Debaters and the rest of the class that everything is negotiable. This will allow open season on one of your most prized possessions— your sanity.

Giving in too much to Debaters can result in other children feeling like you are playing favorites, and can also lead to you trying to balance favors. For example: I let [Debater] have her way last time, so this time I will make her wait. Trying to keep an ongoing tally of who got what when is too complicated and exhausting.

Oh, one last thought: try not to sit them next to Manipulators. The two in collusion is a wild mix.

A sanity kit for the teachers of Competitors

Motto: "Fight to the death!"

Competitors:

- are competitive to the nth degree,
- disregard consequences,
- are defiant in the extreme,
- must win at any cost,
- love to boast,
- can be world-beaters, but can also be lonely "sponges" for attention who rely on that, and
- don't often consider the feelings of others.

One great example is the former cycling champion, Lance Armstrong (see Chapter 5 for more examples).

Common strengths	Common vulnerabilities
- Setting and achieving goals. - Planning. - Creating an advantage (though it's often over others). - Are strong-minded and determined. - Often manage time well. - Can achieve amazing things when they set their mind to it.	- Having a power battle with these kids is like entering an international arms race. - Indomitable and defiant, and will do anything rather than lose face. They will pretend not to care. - Will continue the behavior even when it goes against their interests because they are so entrenched in the need to win.

Helping Competitors to change

Congratulations! You have a highly motivated, firing-on-all-cylinders, exceptional, competitive young person in your class who can easily be engaged by setting him challenges. Unfortunately, he also can't stand to lose.

I recently visited a school that had a time-out room. There was a boy sitting quietly in there so I walked in and, after introducing myself, asked him why he was in time-out. He gave me a steely, don't-mess-with-me kind of look and then replied cheerily, "I'm doing it on credit." This kid was just waiting for the day when a teacher would instruct him to go to time-out, so he could reply, "Already done it!" He was going to win at any cost.

The bluster and power of Lances can mislead you into thinking they are strong. They are driven and sometimes very stressed people. Their fragility, if they do not win, can be quite surprising.

Most bright kids do best with consistency and routines, and Competitors are no exception. Don't back yourself into a corner with these kids. Be able to clearly state the routine: "You know we complete half an hour of reading before we do …"

As Competitors are naturally motivated to achieve, find something meaningful for them to do. This can be used as an inducement to complete other activities, e.g., "If you can finish that essay to a standard I'm happy with, you can do [whatever the activity is] for ten minutes." Notice that the offer was not framed in terms of time. If you say to little Lance, "Finish that in ten minutes and then … ," they'll give you any old rubbish. Emphasize quality, not time or quantity. If you ask them to write 50 words on something, they will give you precisely 50 words—no more, no less.

If you have a few Competitors in your class, try to create situations or learning environments where they can experience failure without feeling ashamed. Absurd quizzes, estimation and "guesstimation" games, and self-scoring charting of progress are some ways of achieving this.

A sanity kit for the teachers of Dare Devils

Motto: "No fear!"

Dare Devils:

- are high sensation-seekers,
- love a challenge, thrills, and excitement,
- are spontaneous, high-impact adrenaline junkies,
- often have limps, bandages, or plaster casts due to scrapes, cuts, and bruises, and
- are not usually gifted with the art of forward planning.

One great example is Steve Irwin, the late, fearless Crocodile Hunter (see Chapter 6 for more examples).

Common strengths	Common vulnerabilities
<ul><li>Sweet-natured and kind.</li><li>Fearless—will try out things that make the rest of us tremble in fear.</li><li>Heaps of energy.</li><li>When task-focused, can accomplish a lot in a short amount of time.</li></ul>	<ul><li>Get lost a lot.</li><li>Not good at assessing risks.</li><li>Don't always learn from their mistakes.</li><li>Not good at deciding not to do things.</li><li>So optimistic that they overestimate their own abilities.</li></ul>

Helping Dare Devils to change

Congratulations! You have a high-voltage, switched-on, determined, energy-to-burn type of kid in your class who will have a go at most things. You may also need to re-think your ideas about class excursions.

And welcome to the world of time trials! Whereas competitive kids can be engaged through challenges, Dare Devils need time trials. Dare Devils can really enjoy school: it can give them the challenges, the peer connections, and the physical activity they thrive on. The bigger issue is whether you will enjoy teaching them, as this can be either a recipe for exhaustion or a delight.

The most powerful behavior-management strategy I've ever seen for these kids is an audible timer. Say, "You've got five minutes to ask ten people about these fifteen different things ..."—and the Dare Devils will rocket out of their seats and into action.

If you can rid your classroom of clocks, it's even more powerful. Without a clock in a classroom, a five-minute time trial can last 20 minutes.

Dare Devils need structure and procedures, but be prepared for them to be tested, as this can become the challenge. Have just a few key rules, otherwise you'll end up in a morass of battle and confusion.

When Dare Devils get a rush of adrenaline, you have a choice: calm them down or navigate their energy. Calming down is not something Dare Devils are naturally skilled at. Nevertheless, it's a skill they can use over and over again. Have quiet areas in your classroom for this purpose.

Navigating the energy of Dare Devils is achieved through trial and error. Look for positive rewards and areas of responsibility. Use computer games for times when Dare Devils have an adrenaline rush. Use physical games on the playground, body math (i.e., using clapping or song or some other rhythm to remember tables and sums by touching various parts of the body), and theater sports with literacy.

The golden rule for teaching Dare Devils is: *when they are disruptive, move them*. Don't wait for them to calm themselves down; they won't.

Dare Devils can be slow to develop an internal world: they are not naturally inclined to reflect on the meaning of things. For this reason, they can become quite upset or unhappy and have no idea why. Or they can be astounded that adults see them as high risk-takers who they wouldn't consider taking on an excursion. Dare Devils may also have very little inkling of how friends or peers feel about things.

During calm moments, helping Dare Devils to consider events from others' perspectives or wondering with them what other people might feel is valuable. Asking them to describe and rate their own feelings also helps. Teaching Dare Devils planning and sequencing skills advantages them greatly. Take an area of their interest and develop a project that requires them to devise and implement a series of sequential steps: this will develop skills that will remain with them for life.

Dare Devils (as well as Competitors) particularly benefit when you include a resilience and emotional intelligence program in your class lessons.

Try to teach Dare Devils the "Stop, Think, Do" method, which is based on traffic lights:

- **Red:** Stop what you are doing.
- **Yellow:** Think about some alternatives.
- **Green:** Select a behavior and do it.

The other really valuable skill to teach Dare Devils is the art of prediction and risk assessment. Use hypothetical situations, role plays, and segments of TV shows, and ask them, "What might happen next? What risks can you see?"

A sanity kit for the teachers of Passive Resisters

Motto: "Problem? What problem?"

Passive Resisters:

- are secretive and private about their thoughts and feelings,
- can seem to be out of touch with their surroundings,
- often lose possessions,
- appear not to listen or take in information,
- can be hard to get going,
- often isolate themselves, and
- can spend endless hours in the library reading, and generally avoiding human interaction.

One great example is the former Indian leader, Mahatma Gandhi, who achieved national independence through noncompliance (see Chapter 7 for more examples).

Common strengths	Common vulnerabilities
- Thoughtful. - Creative. - Sensitive. - Imaginative. - Clever. - Astute.	- Difficult to engage them in a discussion about their thoughts or feelings. - Minimalistic. - Placid and noncommittal. - Communication can boil down to "What?," "Dunno," "As if ...," and "Whatever."

Helping Passive Resisters to change

Congratulations! You have a sensitive, clever, astute young person in your class who will rarely, if ever, show you much direct confrontation or defiance. The downside is that you might tear your hair out trying to work out what this child is thinking about or trying to get her to focus on a task.

Passive Resister kids are vague and disorganized. The "Lost and Found" section of your school is a diagnostic bin for these children.

Passive Resisters will happily sit on the sidelines of your class for years. It is easy to mistake their withdrawal for a lack of interest and motivation. Make a point of noticing them. Personalize your relationship with them. While it's always a good idea to devote five minutes each day to catching up individually with a student one-on-one, this is especially true with Passive Resisters.

Passive Resisters are easily overlooked, either because they are so quiet or because they take so long to assemble an answer to any question. When they stumble over an answer, allow them more time, but keep coming back to them. Don't let them get away with not communicating.

An easy trap for teachers working with Passive Resisters is to do everything for them. Help is not always helpful; in fact it can disempower them. Delegating tasks or areas of responsibility to these kids is a useful way of involving them.

Passive Resisters want to "grow down" rather than grow up. Look for opportunities for these kids to be involved in cross-age tutoring and reading programs with younger students—this often helps them to flourish.

Increase the amount of group work in classes with Passive Resisters. Rotate leadership roles within the groups, and use this to build their confidence in their ability to do and to complete tasks. One teacher who had a lot of this type of bright kid in her class went to the extent of writing on the board key phrases to assist social interaction, such as, "What is the first thing we need to do?" and "What do we need to do next?" and so on.

Having a clear, positive communication system with Passive Resisters' parents is essential. Try to use email or text messaging as a regular strategy for parent communication, where parents have access to these.

Yikes! My class has all of the above!

If you think your class contains children who can be as manipulative as Angelica, negotiate as well as Bart Simpson, debate a point with the aplomb of Margaret Thatcher, show the competitiveness of Winston Churchill, with a blast of Dare Devil combined with a smidgin of Gandhi's passive resistance—don't despair. There are still ways of making your classroom a harmonious learning place, but it is going to take a bit of thinking and strategic planning to get there.

When I work with schools or communities, I often begin by roughly categorizing the young people into four main groups:

1. the high-fliers,
2. the not-switched-on,
3. the switched-off, and
4. the at-risk.

As we go through them, it will become easy to see where each bright kid in your class fits in.

1. The high-fliers

These are the students in your class who cause you little grief. They are "bright-eyed and bushy-tailed," always ready to answer a question or tackle a new problem. High-fliers are almost never a behavioral problem. Bright kids who can appear in this group include Manipulators, Debaters, Passive Resisters, and, very occasionally, a Negotiator.

High-fliers are great kids but, paradoxically, this group also includes your least resilient learners. High-fliers are prone to perfectionism and, when that takes hold of them, they can be reluctant to try new approaches to learning or attempt problems they are unsure of.

Read over Chapter 27, on perfectionism. Also, keep challenging this group of students. Make sure they grapple with thousands of problems, estimation games, and quizzes.

2. The not-switched-on

These are the students in your class who have mastered the art of invisibility, the under-the-radar lifestyle. They can be so unobtrusive that some days you wonder if they are there at all. In large schools these are the students who can spend years doing little more than dodging questions, evading answers, and shirking work. These students are rarely if ever behavioral problems in a school, but they are not exactly contributors, either.

Bright kids that may join the not-switched-on group include:

- Competitors rejuvenating between victories,
- Dare Devils recovering from their latest exploits,
- Passive Resisters hanging out quietly, and
- some of the more well-mannered Negotiators.

3. The switched-off

These are your behavioral problems. These are the look-you-up-and-down, come-on-I-dare-you, how-far-do-you-want-to-take-this types of characters. These are the students who can take you into a battle that will turn you into a shaking, stressed-out mess. Don't go there!

Bright kids who might participate in the switched-off group include:

- disgruntled Manipulators,
- Negotiators summoning an audience for their latest prank,
- Dare Devils executing their latest thrill-seeking adventure,
- Passive Resisters who are stressed, and
- Competitors who are taking you to task.

Even Debaters can join this group for a short time, though usually only to defend their peers against the perceived injustices that you have apparently inflicted on them.

4. The at-risk

At-risk students can include children and young people with significant learning disorders, often coming from homes with significant dysfunction, and often with substantial impulse control and attention issues as well. These students will need individually tailored plans to assist them, and you will require specialized support to have them thrive in your class.

I suggest that teachers list on a piece of paper the names of the students in each group. The percentage of your class that fits into each group will vary from time to time. Students can also shift between groups.

Okay, I've worked out who is in each group—what do I do now?

The top priority for any teacher wanting to restore sanity and harmony to a classroom has to be the not-switched-on. The not-switched-on are passengers, not participants.

As a first step, consider establishing a plan to switch on three not-switched-on students. Set work tasks that you know will appeal to their interest areas. Look through this book for ideas to help you. Use that time-honored teaching combination of fear, distraction, and bribery if you have to. Get them onside and on-task.

Switching on the not-switched-on provides you with a critical mass of pro-learning students. Without this critical mass, classrooms simply become holding bins for behavioral dramas rather than learning places.

Prevalence of each type of bright student

Now you might be thinking, "Surely we should start with the switched-off—they are the ones creating the mayhem and behavioral problems, aren't they?" Let me tell you a few important things about the switched-off:

Distribution of student groups

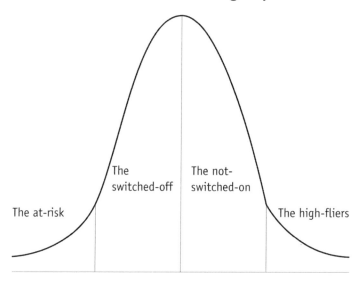

- You can spend the rest of your precious life trying to convert some of them and fail.

- You are not their role model, the peer group is.

- They are not stupid. In fact, many switched-off kids are razor-sharp. One switched-off kid said, "You want to know how to get a day off around here? All you have to do is go to that teacher over there and tell him to go and [have sex]." Not his exact words, but you get the meaning.

- They have learned that one of the easy ways to gain popularity among their peers is to give you a tough time.

- If the bulk of the peer group is engaged in a learning task, some of them (but not all) will change sides and become engaged learners.

In helping bright kids to become engaged and resilient learners, use routines rather than words whenever you can. Use the information in this supplement and in the rest of this book to devise cunning plans to keep one step ahead of them.

Good luck!

Author's notes

Page 2 If you'd like to discuss strategies and ideas, please go to the discussion forum at www.andrewfuller.com.au.

Page 5 **"There is very good research that tells us that the small rituals that we put into family life are a powerful positive force.":** Wolin, S. and Wolin, S. (1995) "Resilience among youth growing up in substance-abusing families," *Pediatric Clinics of North America*, 42, 2, 415–429.

Page 7 **"… an adult outside their family who likes them.":** Fuller, A., McGraw, K., and Goodyear, M. (1999) "Bungy-Jumping Through Life: what young people say promotes wellbeing and resilience," *Australian Journal of Guidance and Counselling*, 9, 1, 159–168.

Page 9 **"What happens just before going to sleep gets processed into long-term dreams.":** Stickgold, R., Hobson, J.A., and Fosse, M. (2001) "Sleep, Learning and Dreams: Off-line memory processing", *Science*, 294, November 2, 1052–1057.

Page 41 Apologies to Steve Irwin, who carefully planned his wonderful exploits. This description is intended to reflect his daring rather than to imply he didn't plan well.

Page 42 **"About 15 percent of children are fearless …":** Loeber, R., Burke, J.D., Lahey, B.B., Winters, A., & Zera, M. (2000) "Oppositional defiant and conduct disorder: a review of the past 10 years," *Journal of the American Academy of Child and Adolescent Psychiatry*, 39, 12, 1468–1484.

Page 47 No disrespect is intended to the wonderful memory of Mahatma Gandhi, who was, of course, highly organized as well as extremely effective as an agent of world change.

Page 51 **"There is a time in many children's lives when they would prefer to 'grow down' rather than grow up.":** The concept of "growing down" rather than up comes from the wonderful work of Australian family therapist, Michael White.

Page 56 **"We have probably learned more in the past few years about the way people learn and develop than we have in the previous 50 years.":** For a full discussion of this area, see Fraiberg, S.H. (1959) *The Magic Years: Understanding and handling the problems of early childhood.* Simon and Schuster: New York.

Page 58 **"The family is … the place where gifts are received, gifts that take a lifetime to unwrap.":** Gopnik, A., Meltzoff, A., and Kuhl, P. (1999) *How babies think*, Weidenfeld and Nicolson: London.

Page 58 **"It is estimated that a four-year-old asks a 'why' question every two-and-a-half minutes!":** Tizard, B., Hughes, M., Pinkerton, G., & Carmichael, H. (1982) "Adults' cognitive demands at home and at nursery school," *Journal of Child Psychology and Psychiatry*, 23, 2, 105.

Page 61 **"The human brain attains 90 percent of its adult weight between four and eight years of age.":** Giedd, J.N., Snell, J.W., Lange, J.C., Rajapakse, B.J., Casey, B.J., Kozuch, P.L., Vaituzis, A.C., Vauss, Y.C., Hamburger, S.D., Kaysen, D., and Rapoport, J.L. (1996) "Quantitative magnetic resonance imaging of human brain development: ages 4 to 18," *Cerebral Cortex*, 6, 551–560.

Page 61 **"Girls exhibiting these problems at this age do worse long term than boys.":** See Cairns, R.B., & Cairns, B.D. (1984) *Lifelines and Risks: Pathways of youth in our time*, Cambridge UP; and Elliott, D.S. (1994) "Serious Violent

Offenders: Onset, developmental course and termination," Presidential address to the American Society of Criminology, 1993, *Criminology*, 32, 1–21.

Page 65 "**Three of the big skills required for success in school ... can be developed with the help of parents.**": Levine, M. (2002) *A Mind at a Time*, Simon and Schuster: New York. And Fuller, A. *Help Your Child Succeed at School*, Inyahead Press: Queenscliff.

Page 67 "**Early maturers score slightly higher on IQ tests than their later-maturing counterparts, and this small advantage appears to persist into adulthood.**": Newcombe, N., and Dubas, J.S. (1989) "Individual differences in cognitive ability: are they related to the timing of puberty?," Lerner, R.M., Foch, T.T. (Eds.) *Biological-psychological-interactions in early adolescence*, Hilldale, NJ: Lawrence Erlbaum and Associates.

Page 68 "**Late-developing boys and early-developing girls are most likely to have trouble.**": Nottlemann, E. D., Susman, E., Inoff-Germain, G., Cutler, G., Loriaux, D., and Chrouros, G. (1987) "Developmental Processes in early adolescence: relationships between adolescent adjustment problems & chronological age, pubertal status & puberty-related serum hormone levels," *Journal of Pediatrics*, 110: 473–480.

Page 71 "**As many as 30,000 synapses may be lost per second over the entire cortex in the early adolescent brain leading to an ultimate loss of almost one half of the synapses that were present in the pre-adolescent period. All this helps with refinement and specialisation.**": Spear, L.P. (2000) "Neurobehavioral Changes in Adolescence," *Current Directions in Psychological Science*, 9, 4, 111–114. See also Spear, L.P. (2000) "The adolescent brain and age-related behavioral manifestations," *Neuroscience and Biobehavioral Reviews*, 24, 417–463.

Page 72 "**Jerome Bruner has suggested that the reason humans are dependent for so long is so they can learn about their specific social environment.**": Cited in Gopnik, A., Meltzoff, A., & Kuhl, P. (1999) *How Babies Think*, Weidenfeld & Nicholson, London.

Page 73 "**Susan Greenfield estimates that over the course of history the size of frontal lobe in humans has increased by 29 percent, compared with 17 percent in chimpanzees and 3 percent in cats.**": Greenfield, S. (1997) *The Human Brain: a guided tour*, Basic Books: New York.

Page 76 "**The research indicating the level of myelination in the cingulate also points to solving the mystery of some family interactions.**": Damasio, A.R. (2000) *Decartes' Error: Emotion, reason and the human brain*, Quill, New York.

Page 76 "**As neuroscientist Linda Spear points out, most species show an alteration in social behavior around the time of adolescence.**": Spear, L.P. (2000) "The adolescent brain and age-related behavioral manifestations," *Neuroscience and Biobehavioral Reviews*, 24, 417–463.

Page 77 "**During an average week, adolescents have been reported to spend close to one-third of their time awake talking with peers, but only 8 percent talking with adults.**": Csikszentimihalyi, M., Larson, R., and Prescott, S.(1977) "The ecology of adolescent activity and experience," *Journal of Youth and Adolescence*, 6, 281–294.

Page 77 "**The decision-making ability of adolescents may be more vulnerable to disruptions by the stresses and strains of everyday living than that of adults.**": Allen, M.T., and Matthews, K.A. (1997) "Hemodynamic responses to laboratory stressors in children and adolescents: the influences of age, race and gender," *Psychophysiology*, 34, 329–339.

Page 77 "The more negative life events an adolescent has, the more likely he is to engage in problem behaviors and the less likely he is to engage in a wide range of positive activities.": Maggs, J.L., Almieda, D.M., and Galambos, N.L. (1995) "Risky business: the paradoxical meaning of problem behavior for young adolescents," *Journal of Early Adolescence*, 15, 344–362.

Page 77 "Adolescents display considerably poorer cognitive performance under time-limited situations than under optimal test conditions.": Dahl, R.E. (2004) "Adolescent Brain Development: A Period of Vulnerabilities and Opportunities," *Annual New York Academy of Science*, 1021, 1–22.

Page 78 "In one study, 80 percent of 11-and-a-half- to 15-year-olds exhibited one or more problem behaviors in a month, such as disobeying parents, school misconduct, substance use, and antisocial acts, including theft or fighting.": Dahl, R.E. (2004) "Adolescent Brain Development: A Period of Vulnerabilities and Opportunities," *Annual New York Academy of Science*, 1021, 1–22.

Page 79 "After peer substance use, perceived levels of stress most strongly predict adolescent alcohol and drug use.": Yurgelen-Todd, D.(1998) "Brain and psyche seminar," Whitehead Institute for Biomedical Research, Cambridge MA, June 11.

Page 80 **Pathway 1: Sailing through:** Harter, S. (1990) "Causes, correlates and the functional role of global self-worth: a life-span perspective" in J.Kollogian and R. Sternberg (Eds.) *Perceptions of Competence and Incompetence across the Life Span*, New Haven, Yale Uni Press.

Page 80 **Pathway 2: Puberty troubles:** Eccles, J.S. & Buchanan, C.M. (1996) "School Transitions In Early Adolescence: What Are We Doing to Our Young People?," in Graber, Julia A., & Petersen, A.C. (Eds.) (1996) *Transitions Through Adolescence-Interpersonal Domains and Context*, Marwah, NJ, Lawrence Erlbaum.

Page 81 **Pathway 3: Mid-adolescent conniptions:** Moffit, T. E., (1993), "Adolescence limited & life course persistent antisocial behavior: a developmental taxonomy," *Psychological Review*, 100, 674–701.

Page 81 **Pathway 4: Turnaround:** Compas, B., (1995), "Adolescent Development: Pathways of Risk and Resilience," *Annual Review of Psychology*, 46, 265–93.

Page 86 "It makes people less flexible and it makes it harder for bright kids to change their moods.": Gould, E. (2004) "Stress, Deprivation and adult neuro-genesis" in M. Gazzaniga (Ed) *The Cognitive Neurosciences*, Bradford: Cambridge.

Page 88 "That's why you sometimes get monosyllabic grunts, especially from teenagers.": Bunsey, M., and Eichenbaum, H. (1996) "Conservation of hippocampal memory function in rats and humans," *Nature*, 379, 255–257.

Page 88 "Fluorescent lighting has been associated with elevated levels of cortisol.": London, W. (1988) "Brain/Mind Bulletin Collections," *New Sense Bulletin*, 13, April, 7c; Harmon, D.B. (1991) "The Coordinated Classroom" in Liberman, J. *Light: Medicine of the future*, Bear and Co Publishing: Sante Fe; and Heschong Mahone Group (1999) "Day Lighting in Schools: an investigation into the relationship between day lighting and human performance," submitted to George Loisos, The Pacific Gas and Electric Company on behalf of the California Board for Energy Efficiency Third-Party Program.

Page 89 "Dopamine is good for pleasure and motivation: it's the party animal of the neuro-chemical world.": Schultz, J.M. (2002) "Getting formal with dopamine and reward," *Neuron*, 36, 241–263; Schultz, J.M., Dayan, P., and Montague, P.R. (1997) "A neural substrate of prediction and reward," *Science*,

275, 1593–1599; and Fiorillo, C.D., Tobler, P.N., and Schultz, W. (2003) "Discrete coding of reward probability and uncertainty by dopamine neurons," *Science*, 299, 1898–1902.

Page 89 "**There is evidence that some families may have patterns where they have difficulties with this.**": Gazzaniga, M.S. (2004) *The Cognitive Neurosciences* III, MIT Press, London.

Page 89 "**... dietary supplements of tyrosine and Omega 3 and 6, which have also been associated with increases in dopamine.**": Ross, J., (2002) *The Mood Cure*, Thorsons: London.

Page 93 "**In order to help children to sleep well, lower the lighting of an evening in your home or use indirect lighting such as lamps.**": Fuller, A. (2006) unpublished research.

Page 94 "**If a bright kid is getting only five or six hours of sleep, she loses the last two REM cycles, and thereby reduces the amount of time the brain has to consolidate information into long-term storage.**": Foster, R., and Kreitzman, L. (2004) *Rhythms of Life: the biological clocks that control the daily lives of every living thing*, Profile: London.

Page 94 "**Having a nap can be just as effective in promoting learning and memory as a full night's sleep.**": Mednick, S., Nakayama, K., and Stickgold, R. (2003) "Sleep-dependent learning: a nap is a good as a night," *Nature Neuroscience*, 6, 7, 697–698.

Page 95 "**... if you sleep from 10 p.m. to 7 a.m., the mid-point of your sleep is 2:30 a.m., which means that around 2:30 p.m. is your most likely downtime.**": Restak, R . (2001) *Mozart's Brain and the Fighter Pilot*, Harmony: New York.

Page 96 "**Fluorescent light raises cortisol levels in the bloodstream and can suppress the immune system.**": London, W.(1988) "Brain/Mind Bulletin Collections," *New Sense Bulletin*, 13, April, 7c; and Harmon, D.B. (1991) "The Coordinated Classroom" in Liberman, J. *Light: Medicine of the future*, Sante Fe, NM: Bear and Co Publishing.

Page 96 "**A 150- to 200-watt globe equals 2500 lux, and there is evidence that using a bright light in the day improves mood.**": Heschong Mahone Group (1999) "Day lighting in schools: an investigation into the relationship between day lighting and human performance," submitted to George Loisos, The Pacific Gas and Electric Company on behalf of the California Board for Energy Efficiency Third-Party Program.

Page 97 "**Julia Ross ... writes about the importance of increasing proteins and lessening carbohydrates at breakfast time.**": Ross, J. (2002) *The Mood Cure*, Thorsons: London.

Page 98 "**Some studies have related Mozart's music to increased intelligence levels ...**": Malyarenko, T.N., Kuraev, G.A., Malyarenko, Yu.E., Khvatovas, M.V., Romanova, N.G., and Gurina, V.I.. (1996) "The development of brain electric activity in 4-year-old children by long-term stimulation with music," *Human Physiology*, 22, 76–81.

Page 98 "**...the clarinet, piano, and advanced guitar require fine motor skills, whereas the trumpet, drums, and percussion require gross motor skills.**": Levine, M. (2002) *A Mind at a Time*, New York: Simon and Schuster.

Page 99 "**Twenty-two percent watch television for more than three hours a day, and 14 percent also spend more than three hours playing computer games.**": Fuller, A. (2006) unpublished research.

Page 99 "... a study of over 1,000,000 students in Israel found the relationship between TV viewing and educational attainment to be complex.": Razel, M. (2001) "The Complex Model of Television Viewing and Educational Achievement," *The Journal of Educational Research*, 94, 6, 371–379.

Page 102 "**Author Jeff Conley has a wonderful expression ...**": Conley, J. (1999) *Habits of the Heart*, Book Partners: Oregon.

Page 127 "**Household cleanliness may not ... but in surveys of parents it regularly comes up as one of the biggest issues facing parents on a day-to-day basis.**": Fuller, A. (2002) *Raising Real People*, ACER Press, Melbourne.

Page 132 "**About one in three kids habitually worries.**": Muris, P., Meesters, C., Merckelbach, H., Sermon, A., & Zwakhalen, S. (1998) "Worry in Normal Children," *Journal of the American Academy of Child and Adolescent Psychiatry*, 37, 7, 703.

Page 148 "**It is estimated that people think an average of 13,000 thoughts every day.**": Charlie Greer in "What are you thinking?" cites statistics of 12,000–50,000 thoughts daily on average. See http://www.hvacprofitboosters.com/Tips/Tip_Archive/tip_archive7.html.

Page 150 "**Generally, research indicates that ... we are, if anything, slightly less happy than we were 50 years ago.**": R. Veenhoven, World Database of Happiness—Trend in Nations, Erasmus University, Rotterdam. Available at www.worlddatabaseofhappiness.eur.nl/trendnat.

Page 152 Graph from Csikzentmihalyi, M., 1990, *Flow: The psychology of happiness*, Rider Press, London.

Page 157 "**If, as it is estimated, 70 percent of the jobs that will exist in the year 2020 don't exist yet ...**": Ellyard, P. (2001) *Ideas for the New Millennium*, Melbourne UP.

Page 165 "**Basically, the picture is that more young people today than ever before experience depression, and they begin feeling depressed at younger and younger ages.**": Birmaher, B., Ryan, N.D., Williamson, B.A., Brent, D.A., and Kaufman, J. (1996) "Childhood and Adolescent Depression: A Review of the Past 10 Years, Part II," *Journal of the American Academy of Child and Adolescent Psychiatry*, 35, 12, 1575– 1582.

Page 167 "**By at least four years of age, they know that it is wrong to mislead someone but they don't really understand why it is wrong.**": Ekman, P. (1989) *Why Kids Lie: how parents can encourage truthfulness*, Schwartz and Wilkinson: Melbourne.

Page 169 Table adapted from Ekman, 1989 and expanded.

Page 173 "**A survey of school students about words they associate with popularity is revealing.**": Fuller, A. (2005) Unpublished survey of school students in Perth.

Page 185 "**Traditional healing**": I am grateful to Ian Gawler for sharing this knowledge with me.

Teachers' Supplement
I am grateful to many teachers for sharing their experiences.

Page 207 "**One switched-off kid said, 'You want to know how ... tell him to go and [have sex].'**": I am particularly thankful to Esme Murphy for sharing this story.

Acknowledgements

I am extremely lucky to be surrounded and supported by a wonderful group of people who are much cleverer than I am and who are able to politely curb my wilder ideas. I'd particularly like to thank Anthony Beardall, Bob Bellhouse, Lorraine Day, Mary Duma, Lucy Fuller, Sam Fuller, Vicki Fuller, Brenda Hosking-Brown, Glenda Johnston, Karen McGraw, Chris Miller, Esme Murphy, Michele Silva-Cummin, and Kerry Winchester for their great assistance. You are all marvels!

For turning my clumsily-phrased manuscript into a fantastic book, I relied on the masterful minds and patient personalities of Sean Doyle, Rex Finch, and Adrian Osborne.

Reading list

Csikszentmihalyi, M. (1990) *Flow: The psychology of happiness*, Rider Press, London.

Ekman, P. (1989) *Why Kids Lie: How parents can encourage truthfulness*, Schwartz and Wilkinson, Melbourne.

Fraiberg, S.H. (1959) *The Magic Years: Understanding and handling the problems of early childhood*, Simon and Schuster, New York.

Fuller, A. (2002) *Raising Real People*, ACER, Melbourne.

Fuller, A. (2004) *Help Your Child Succeed at School*, Inyahead Press, Queenscliff (www.inyahead.com.au).

Gallway, W.T. (1974) *The Inner Game of Tennis*, Pan, London.

Greene, R.W. and Ablon, J.S. (2006) *Treating Explosive Kids*, Guildford, New York.

Healy, J.M. (1998) *Failure to Connect: How computers affect our children's minds—and what we can do about it*, Simon and Schuster, New York.

Kageler, L. (1989) *Helping Your Teenager Cope with Peer Pressure*, Family Tree, Colorado.

Kurcinka, M.S. (1991) *Raising Your Spirited Child*, Harper, New York.

Levine, M. (2002) *A Mind at a Time*, Simon and Schuster, New York.

Levy, R. and O'Hanlon, B. (2001) *Try and Make Me!: Simple strategies that turn off the tantrums and create cooperation*, Rodale, New York.

Marshall, M. (2004) *Discipline without Stress, Punishment or Rewards*, Piper Press, California.

Nelson, J. (1981) *Positive Discipline*, Ballantine, New York.

Wallace, I. (1996) *You and Your ADD Child: Practical strategies for coping with everyday problems*, Harper Collins, Sydney.

Index